Praise for *Yes! Your Child Can*

"Creativity is important in every walk of life, mine especially. And Vicki Waller's book, *Yes! Your Child Can: Creating Success for Children with Learning Differences*, shows what an extraordinary and creative educational therapist she is. She digs deep to find out what interests each child, unlocks their own creativity focusing on a subject a child is passionate about, and, astonishingly, they learn to read. Magic happens!"

—**Michael D. Eisner**, former chairman and CEO of the Walt Disney Company and president of The Tornante Company

"If you have a feeling that your child is not quite on top of things, that your child is not well understood at school or even at home, that your child could be doing so much better if only. . . *Yes! Your Child Can* completes the 'if only. . .' Dr. Waller is my favorite kind of expert. She totally knows her stuff. She's seen a lot of kids, like a lot. And she knows how to get to the bottom of things. Plus, she loves children. Like a detective, she loves figuring out what makes children tick, especially the ones who tick differently from most. She's the person I'd send my own child to, if I needed help, because she's seen it all. She knows how to tell a parent what the parent really needs, with no extra fluff or theory. If you're not lucky enough to get a session with Dr. Waller in person, then this book is the next best thing. It's an instant classic. And the title says it all: YES!"

—**Edward Hallowell, M.D.**, author of *Driven to Distraction* and *A.D.H.D. 2.0*

"Dr. Waller unlocks the super powers within her students using their own creativity to make their learning soar."

—**Patty Jenkins**, writer/director, *Wonder Woman*

"Dr. Waller is a force of nature and a gift to people like me who learn differently. She is a brilliant educator for those of us who the system readily discards. Her heart is gold and her enthusiasm for lifting people up who learn differently or who were not born on a level playing field is platinum. For over 20 years serving on the board of the Putney Open-Door Fund, a nonprofit that offers full scholarships to students from underserved communities enabling them to participate in educational programs all over the world, she has changed lives and opened opportunities for many. If we could clone Dr. Waller, the world would be a better place."

—**Peter Shumlin**, former governor of Vermont

"This is by far the best book on learning differences I have ever read. It is comprehensive, readable, so wise, beautifully balanced between anecdotes about the kids Dr. Waller has worked with and her terrific recommendations and advice. Dr. Waller covers all aspects of what a parent will run into dealing with learning differences in her child. This is a brilliant book!"

—**Dana Buchman**, founder, Promise Project

"It has been a great privilege to connect with Dr. Waller and to see firsthand the tremendous care and attention she gives to her students. She has provided numerous students with introductions to me and thus those having an interest in sharks have been able to converse with me about them."

—**Chris Fallows**, shark expert, wildlife photographer, and co-host of Discovery Channel Shark Week

"Dr. Waller is a brilliant, gifted educator who has taught countless children with learning differences to read, thrive, and achieve success. In *Yes! Your Child Can* she provides parents with a step-by-step guide about what to expect when they come to the sudden realization that their smart, interesting child is failing in school. In this groundbreaking book, based on 40 years of teaching children with learning differences and evidence-based research, Dr. Waller shows parents how to create fun learning experiences that enhance a child's unique passions. By teaching to their interests, Dr. Waller engages her students and makes them excited about learning and reading. It is evident in this book that she believes and is enthusiastic about each student's unique talents and strengths. She makes each child feel understood, important and appreciated for who they are. That is a recipe for future success!"

—**Vicky Goodman**, founder and president, Friends of the Semel Institute for Neuroscience and Human Behavior at UCLA, and Resnick Neuropsychiatric Hospital, founding board of directors

"Dr. Waller understands the complexities of children, the importance of reading, and how to bring them together successfully."

—**Kevin Henkes**, Caldecott Medal and Newbury award-winning writer and illustrator of *Kitten's First Full Moon, Lilly's Purple Plastic Purse*, and over 50 other children's books

YES!
Your Child Can

YES!
Your Child Can

Creating Success for Children
with Learning Differences

VICTORIA E. WALLER, Ed.D.

Fresno, California

Yes! Your Child Can

Published by Quill Driver Books, an imprint of Linden Publishing
2006 South Mary Street, Fresno, California 93721
(559) 233-6633 / (800) 345-4447 / QuillDriverBooks.com

Quill Driver Books and colophon are trademarks of Linden Publishing, Inc.

The content of this book is for informational purposes only and is not intended to diagnose, treat, cure, or prevent any condition or disease. You understand that this book is not intended as a substitute for consultation with a licensed practitioner. Please consult with your own physician or healthcare specialist regarding the suggestions and recommendations made in this book. The use of this book implies your acceptance of this disclaimer.

Linden Publishing titles may be purchased in quantity at special discounts for educational, business, or promotional use. To inquire about discount pricing, please refer to the contact information above. For permission to use any portion of this book for academic purposes, please contact the Copyright Clearance Center at www.copyright.com.

ISBN 978-1610353-86-1

135798642

Printed in the United States of America
on acid-free paper.

Cover design by Tanja Prokop
Cover image: Freepik.com
Interior design by Carla Green, Clarity Designworks.
Illustrations courtesy of Carolyn LaPorte

Library of Congress Cataloging-in-Publication Data on file.

Table of Contents

Foreword

A Success Story

When Dr. Waller asked us to write the foreword to this important book, we immediately and emphatically said "Yes!" "We" are the mother of "Kenny," the name Dr. Waller applied to a very real child in her comprehensive book, and "Kenny" himself. Offering a few words about *Yes! Your Child Can* is the least we could do given the life-changing efforts the author had provided us by guiding Kenny to read.

As the introduction explains, this book fills a unique gap among the vast selection of books designed to assist parents with children who struggle to read. In particular, Dr. Waller focuses on children struggling with learning differences who find it difficult to prioritize and complete tasks and have related challenges, yet do have bona fide strengths, interests, talents, and passions. This book draws on decades of rich experiences and shifts the perspective from learning disability to learning *difference*, which is huge.

Everyone learns differently. This book is not snake oil; it does not claim to be a guaranteed remedy, professing wiz-bang results in no time at all. This is a book about creating a whole team to advocate for each child's success, by understanding the multifaceted nature of each young reader's challenges. It provides guidance on how to build students' confidence about what they can do and to improve executive function so that they ultimately become proficient readers and writers.

This book took me, as Kenny's mom, back through the journey. It reminded me of the emotional roller coaster, doubt, guilt, and striving to find the key to unlock his mind. I could sense that Kenny was smart, but he struggled so much in school. Dr. Waller understands and validates that journey and provides countless examples and micro-case studies of real students finding their way to become active—or even voracious—readers.

The book is chock-full of practical lessons learned from managing tough experiences with neuropsychologists, clinical psychologists, developmental pediatricians, teachers, principals, and unsavory fellow students. Yes, there are even a few stories about gaining the confidence needed to deal with bullies.

The book provides helpful and specific strategies to try while also explaining why they work and in which context they are best applied. Dr. Waller also guides readers away from common pitfalls. The text is easy to read, engaging, colorful, and at times humorous and puts front and center the role of empathy in teaching children to read.

Once Dr. Waller allowed me, "Kenny," to believe I was good at something and once she showed me, through the unique methodology laid out in this book, that I was smart, then I became engaged and took charge of my own learning.

As I worked with Vicki, everything began to fall into place for me.

I spent more time organizing my assignments, rereading my work, and allowing extra time for my tests. And after a few years, I was able to be in honors classes in high school in some subjects. I was actually awarded merit-based scholarships throughout my entire educational career (a bachelor's where I was top of my class, then two master's, and a doctorate).

As his mother, I saw Dr. Waller bring out all the potential I knew Kenny had tucked inside. He is now four years post-PhD, a research social scientist who sits on doctoral committees, is an associate editor for a key journal in his field, and is the author of more than 50-peer-reviewed scientific journal articles.

If you know a child struggling with school and learning to read, and you have that "gut feeling" that they are intelligent but not receiving the right instruction, you need to read this book. The sooner you do so, the better the outcome will be.

Karen Ellen Williams Locke (Kenny's Mom)
Woodbury University, Board of Trustees
Amie Karen Cancer Fund, four-term past president
Exceptional Children's Foundation, Honorary Committee

Dexter Henry Locke, PhD, MA, MESc (Kenny)
USDA Forest, Baltimore Field Station, research social scientist
University of Maryland, College Park,
    special member of the Graduate Faculty
Urban Forestry & Urban Greening, Aassociate editor

Introduction

The First Book to Read
If Your Child Has Learning Differences

"You don't have to be 'Magic' to be special.
You're already special. You're you!"
Magic Johnson, former professional basketball player

Magic Johnson, one of the greatest basketball players of all time and now a successful businessman and philanthropist, has learning differences and as a child couldn't read or write. His quote is one of the most important messages I've heard from any famous person with differences. Every child I have taught in over 40 years of working with children with differences was special. They were smart and interesting and had passions and strengths.

The term to describe children with learning differences used to be, mainly, "learning disabilities." But I have always concentrated on children's abilities, not their disabilities. Fortunately, there is now finally a change occurring in the fields of education and medicine to replace the term "learning disabilities" with "learning differences." "Learning differences" acknowledges both the challenges *and* the strengths of these children who are bright and interesting but who may be failing in school.

Six years ago, I began writing a book on the subject, focusing on Alex, one of my students who had learning differences and attention deficit hyperactivity disorder/inattentive (ADHD/Inattentive). I taught Alex, a highly intelligent student, to read and write beginning at the age of seven by using his passion for cooking. After each session, I wrote a summary for his teachers, parents, and other therapists. Thus began a three-year journey with Alex that ended up with a 370-page book about Alex's journey, including stories of other students from my decades of teaching children with learning differences.

But I was stuck. I loved my stories and the success of my students, and I wanted to make sure these stories helped other children, parents, teachers, school administrators, and therapists. Teachers, though they had good intentions, were often not taught how to teach students with learning differences; school administrators tended to clump all students with learning differences into a category of "learning disabled," meaning "not able" to learn in the regular classroom;

and parents were searching for someone to hold their hand and guide them through a very confusing process. Because I did not know how to move the stories into a book, I put my pages away on a shelf in my study.

Over the course of three particular months, three incidents occurred that made me realize I had to finish my book no matter what so I could help readers understand that with the right interventions and guidance, children with learning differences could be highly successful and "make it." My book would be their guide.

This aha moment didn't come all at once. The first incident started one day when the doorbell rang. I opened the door to see a very tall young man.

"Dr. Waller," he said. "Is that you?"

"It's me," I said. "Who are you?"

"You don't remember?" He smiled through his beard. "It's me, Kenny."

And then I knew exactly who it was. I remembered him like it was yesterday, though in reality it had been 23 years ago.

I could still see Kenny in my classroom when he was seven years old, directing claymation films for a solid three hours, like a real Hollywood director. His ideas, scripts, and scenes were all incredible. In the first grade, he was already smart and creative. *And he'd had severe learning differences.*

Back then, Kenny's passion had been directing those claymation films. Though Kenny had been totally misunderstood by his teachers and administrators, he was a star in my reading class. It was easy for him to focus in my class because I taught based on the students' passions. I believed then, and still do, that we can empower students if we focus on their abilities rather than their differences.

"I came here to thank you," Kenny started out. "I just received a doctorate in geography. I went to Yale and Clark and received a master's degree at both universities, and now I'm going for my postdoc. I started to think about how I could have possibly gotten to where I am, and then I remembered." He smiled at me. "It was you. You believed in me, you said I could do anything I set my mind to. But you always said I had to find my passions first." I felt myself tear up. "You and my mom were my only advocates. You knew I was smart. I just wanted to thank you. All my teachers through elementary and high school said I was just an average student, with lots of learning differences and very little focus and should maybe get a job at McDonald's—definitely not go to college."

As I think about that day, I still cry. His mom came by later and told me that Kenny visiting me to say thank you meant more to her than all the degrees he received. Kenny was grateful that someone had believed in him when no one else did.

The second incident happened not too long afterward. I received an email from a mom whose son I had taught seven years before. David was having a Bar Mitzvah and wanted me to hold the Torah because, as he said in his Bar Mitzvah speech, "Vicki was my only friend in second grade. I was different from the other kids. She taught me how to read and helped me pursue my passion. Without her, I wouldn't be who I am today."

David's passion, at six years old, was the *Titanic*. I used that passion to help him learn to read and write. We read and researched everything about the *Titanic*. Finally, after studying about the *Titanic* for weeks, David wrote a letter to Robert Ballard, the man who discovered the wreck of the *Titanic* on the ocean floor. David asked him many questions, and Dr. Ballard actually wrote back! At the end of his letter he wrote, "Dream big, David, and don't let anyone talk you out of your dreams!" David, a voracious reader, is in eighth grade now and walks around with a book in his hands at all times.

The third incident happened at a grandparents' meeting at my grandchild's school. A woman approached me who looked very familiar, but I couldn't place her. "Are you Dr. Waller?"

I nodded. "Yes."

"You saved my child."

This shocked me. "Who is your child?" I asked.

"Elizabeth. She was in your pull-out reading class 17 years ago, and the school kept saying she wasn't smart and maybe needed a special school, and you kept telling me she was very smart and creative, she just couldn't focus. You told us to get her tested to see if she had learning differences."

Her parents took her out of that school because they thought she was "limited." She was tested by a psychologist who specialized in evaluating children with learning differences. The results proved she *was* smart. A psychiatrist who specialized in children with attention issues put her on medication to help her with her attention. She got the help she needed and graduated from USC with honors.

"We were just talking about how you were the one who believed in her and made her feel smart," her mother said.

Elizabeth's passion ever since she was in elementary school was always fashion. She is 25 now and a stylist, dressing movie stars in Hollywood.

These three incidents spanning a few weeks' time meant that I had to finish my book. I needed to be the "voice of hope" for parents going through this journey with their child.

Every parent's conversation with me takes a similar trajectory. They are drowning in information put forth by research-heavy texts or anecdotal evidence, but no one is actually answering their most pressing concerns: "I have a gut feeling something's wrong with my child," most parents tell me at the beginning, "but I can't pinpoint what."

"My child daydreams all of the time," they say, "and he has difficulty forming letters and can't read, but I know he is very smart. Can you help me?"

"The school wants a brain doctor to test my child!" they tell me in desperate emails. "What's wrong with my child's brain? What is a brain doctor? Where do I go for testing?"

"The psychiatrist is suggesting medication, but medication scares me! Is it safe?" they ask.

"My child's teacher doesn't get her. Should I talk to the teacher or let it go?"

This book was written as a response to the countless parents who have begged me to write a straight-talking book that goes beyond jargon and clinical definitions. My mission in writing it is perhaps most similar to Heidi Murkoff and Sharon Mazel's *What to Expect When You're Expecting*, the pregnancy guide that moves you through all stages of pregnancy. My aim is to offer a clear, step-by-step path that helps cut through the overwhelming maze of information and advice.

Yes! Your Child Can is based on the foundational belief that you need to draw out your child's innate intelligence for them to succeed. The book is a guide to identifying your child's learning differences. It provides a complete road map for navigating the complex educational and social systems you'll encounter as you lead your child to a love of reading.

I graduated from the University of Cincinnati with a doctorate in education and a major in learning differences and received the distinguished alumna award several years later. I've taught thousands of children who have been considered "disabled" by their principals, school systems, teachers, and even their own parents. I've taught children who have been tested for a variety of differences to read and write by using a secret sauce: their passions and strengths. Ball pythons, roller coasters, cooking, cars, sharks, the *Titanic*, any usual or unusual subject you could imagine.

In the past decade, I finally began to see a rise in awareness about children with learning differences. Since then, many books have been written, and thousands of blogs, podcasts, websites, and even businesses have popped up, promising miracles in your child's schoolwork in only six weeks for only $6,000. "Do this, and your child will be cured!" With so many ideas all over the Internet, where should parents turn?

I wrote this book so that you would have a good place to turn. Teachers, educational specialists, psychologists, therapists, principals, and administrators can all rely on this book. Education programs in colleges can use the ideas presented here to create courses on how to teach children with

learning differences. These chapters can help absolutely anyone answer the questions about what to expect when you
work with a child with learning differences. But I wrote it,
mostly, for parents.

From teaching thousands of children with learning differences, I have come to understand the trajectory from the
time you have that "gut feeling" that something is amiss to
the diagnosis and all the way to their success as a learner. This
book is your hand to hold through this joyful, and sometimes
painful, journey of discovery. The chapters offer techniques
for confidence building, how to use assistive technology, and
how to handle meltdowns. It provides book lists your child
will love, interview questions you want to make sure you ask
specialists, and maps for handling transitions, all integrated
into a fun, informative narrative. The exercises and activities in reading and writing can be used by parents, teachers,
therapists, and the children themselves to help transform
them into the students they were meant to be. Most of all, it
includes stories of actual children and their challenging journeys to transcend labels that take away their personal power.

By reading this book you will begin to see that your child
can be successful. I'm not saying the journey is an easy one,
but there is no reason that, with the right help, your child
won't become one of the millions of competent and successful people with learning differences. The world today is
run by high-profile people who have succeeded beyond the
world's wildest imaginations, even though they had learning differences, including Henry Winkler, Michael Phelps,
Steven Spielberg, Barbara Corcoran from *Shark Tank*, Richard Branson, astronaut Scott Kelly, Whoopi Goldberg, Bill

Gates, Steve Jobs, and Anderson Cooper, who stated, "I had access to people who taught me with what I was passionate about." Your child's passions are the best way to access your child's aptitude and genius so they can be a successful, happy learner.

The book was also designed to allow you to gain confidence in your own parenting skills and ensure you that a life of productivity and achievement is never beyond your child's reach. While the book entertains and informs, the undercurrent that drives the narrative is *hope*. Let this be your final step in what seems like an endless scavenger hunt, where you'll finally get to open the treasure box of your child's personal genius. Let the journey begin . . .

When Dav Pilkey, author of the *Captain Underpants* and *Dog Man* series, came to Los Angeles for an author visit, I suggested to my students that they go hear him speak. They were totally surprised when he told them his teachers at school had thought he was "behaviorally challenged." Because of his lack of attention and learning differences, the teacher put his desk in the hallway. While he sat in the hallway, he exercised his passion for writing and drawing by making comic books with a superhero called Captain Underpants. His teacher said, "You'd better straighten up, young man, because you can't spend the rest of your life making silly books." Dav's books have sold over 70 million copies in 20 languages!

Now Dav gives some of his own learning differences to the characters in his books. It was an amazing experience for my students to see a very successful writer speak about how he felt in school. My students were enthralled by him. I overheard one student say, "I'm just like him. Maybe I can be a writer, too."

[1]

The Gut Feeling

Shark Tank celebrity investor Barbara Corcoran's mom repeatedly told her that her "disability" was a gift rather than an impairment. Her "gift" allowed Corcoran to problem-solve by using her imagination to fill in the blanks. She turned a $1,000 loan into a $5 billion real estate empire. Barbara says her differences aren't a crutch but a gift, and she's thankful for the ability to use them as a window to success.

——————————————//——————————————

In my over 40 years of working with thousands of children with learning differences, the first thing I hear from a parent is, "I always had a gut feeling something was wrong with my child."

Nine years ago Mitchell and Steve arrived to talk to me about their son, Alex, who, at seven years old, had reading and writing issues. They were in the process of interviewing therapists to see who would be the best fit.

Mitchell told me about his feeling about Alex when we sat down for our first meeting. "Alex is a twin, and from the beginning there were certain differences between him and Billy." He went on to say that Alex never crawled, but his pediatrician had told them that kids often started different activities at different times. "We'd speak to Alex," Mitchell told me. "And even at three years old, he was unresponsive. He'd drift off." Alex's twin had been just ahead of him in growth milestones, but then the spaces became wider and Alex's developmental lags progressed from a month difference between the boys to many months' difference.

EARLY RED FLAGS

Steve went on to tell the history of Alex's life. He said it was scattered with red flags, but they just didn't know exactly what to do. Alex was hard to soothe as a baby. He had difficulty catching a ball, running in a coordinated way, and maintaining balance. When he was four, a doctor evaluated him and told them he was smart, but also found he had challenges with auditory processing and attention. One day the four-year-old twins were in their car seats when Alex's twin, Billy, unbuckled his seat belt. Alex asked if Mitchell would do it for him.

"Why can't you do it yourself?" his twin asked.

Alex replied, "You're older."

Alex already recognized he couldn't do many things his twin could, but being smart, he made the inference that Billy could do more because he was the older twin. In reality, Alex was the older child, by one minute.

Mitchell listed all the interventions they already had done. When Alex was four, they'd gotten occupational therapy to focus on his gross and fine motor skills. In kindergarten he attended speech and language therapy to work on expressive language and language sequencing. In first grade Alex saw a reading specialist. Recently, Alex had started seeing a new speech/language therapist who focused on language processing and expressive language. In the same office Alex was still seeing an occupational therapist for his fine motor, sequencing, and organizational difficulties.

PUTTING IT ALL TOGETHER

Alex wasn't hyperactive. He didn't have any impulse control issues. And he had no frustration, mood, or anxiety symptoms. All his therapists said he was a willing participant in therapy. And he had good friends and good relationships with his three siblings.

"But that feeling is still there," Mitchell told me. "There is something we aren't seeing."

In this case the dads had the gut feeling for a long time and did the correct interventions to help Alex. But they were still missing a puzzle piece.

After seeing Alex for a few weeks, I suggested he get tested by a neuropsychologist. The results were not surprising to me, but they were to the dads. Alex had learning differences and attention deficit hyperactive disorder/inattentive. Most parents think of a child with attention issues as hyperactive. Inattentive is not as easy to diagnose. Alex was very quiet but not paying attention at all. His lack of attention and inability to focus was greatly impacting his ability to succeed. He was put on medication, which greatly improved his ability to focus. He was able to be more productive in all his therapies and began to succeed in learning how to read and write.

That gut feeling almost always signifies a challenge or a difference that is making it tough for a student to succeed. Parents have this gut feeling, not only in the United States but all over the world.

SOMETHING'S NOT QUITE RIGHT

There I was in the summer of 2016 at the top of the Rock of Gibraltar on a trip with my husband when Jonathan, a man from London, asked me what I did for a living. After I told him, he immediately said, "I have a child, Tony, who is exactly like you're describing. Ever since he was two years old, I knew something just wasn't right. My wife said I was crazy. She said he was a normal, active kid."

Jonathan went on to tell me that they had a fence surrounding their property, and even though he was only two years old, his son Tony would start running. He'd run around and around the perimeter of the yard, over and over until they caught him. He ran everywhere. At home and school, he was in constant motion.

The teachers kept telling the parents that Tony was highly active and very creative and would always construct the most amazing sculptures out of plain boxes. In school he couldn't stay focused on regular subjects but could stay focused for hours when he was working on his "box projects." Finally, the principal of the school told the parents she was worried about Tony because although he was definitely smart, she thought he had attention deficit hyperactivity disorder and learning differences. The principal suggested they get Tony tested.

Tony was found to have learning differences and attention deficit, as well as a very high IQ. He was put on medication and, Jonathan told me, is a "highly successful lawyer today."

Jonathan's "feeling" that Tony had abilities but could not access them because of his inattention helped the mom finally realize Tony needed to be tested to see what was wrong. The principal, who had the same feeling, too, helped convince the mom and became an advocate for Tony throughout his years in school. She knew how creative he was and that he was not succeeding because of his inattention and learning differences.

An old friend, Peter, whom I met at a wedding in Italy 20 years ago, visited me two years ago. He began telling me he had concerns about his nephew, but his sister kept saying he was a gifted violinist and couldn't possibly have learning differences, even though he did very poorly in school. I told Peter to convince his sister to have the child tested.

> Smart, talented, creative kids can also be kids with learning differences. Trust your instincts.

A few months after his nephew was tested, I heard from Peter that the tests found he had learning differences. Now

5

the boy is receiving academic help, is successful in school, and is still highly talented with his violin.

Over the years, one thing I have noticed is that often one parent sees how smart or talented their child is, but they also understand that something, somehow, is just not right. However, the other parent or family member will feel strongly that nothing is wrong.

"He'll snap out of it," a highly anxious mom told me when she called after her seven-year-old son was tested for learning differences.

For many years, I have taught children diagnosed with these differences and, unfortunately, they do not "snap out of it." If they succeed in school, it is often because their parents don't deny the issues but follow the professional's suggestions on how to help their child.

If you picked up this book because you had a strong feeling about your child, there's a chance you have googled everything, and because you feel overwhelmed, you may hope your child will "snap out of it." This is very normal. You are frustrated, afraid, and sad about the journey your sweet, loving, smart child, who is failing in school, has had to endure. This book was written for you.

THE TAKEAWAY

Remember to:

- Start to shift your thinking and try to accept who your child is today and what they *can* do.

- Try to get the best help available, starting with the information in this book. Know that with good interventions, your child has every chance in the world to succeed. In Alex's case, his parents had him doing many therapies early on. But the most important missing part was that Alex was ADHD/inattentive, making it hard for him to listen and learn.

- Act on that gut feeling as soon as it appears, rather than thinking your child will snap out of it. This is true even when your child is young.

Early intervention is extremely important. If you have those gut feelings and are reading this book, you have taken the first step in getting the help your child needs to succeed.

[2]

The Importance of
Early Intervention

Film director, producer, and screenwriter Steven Spielberg grew up with learning differences. He has said his teachers thought he wasn't studying hard enough and he was lazy. In fact, he just needed to find the right thing to apply his strengths to.

———————— // ————————

Something parents almost always say to me when they first call me about their child is, "My child has some difficulties in school, but I'm sure will snap out of it." Unfortunately, their child will not "snap out of it."

Two years ago, when Jack was in first grade, his mom, Alice, called me. "I got your name from a friend who told me you were great at teaching children to read," she told me. "My son is in first grade and can't read. The teacher says he can't focus in class and has difficulty with writing and putting his thoughts on paper." Alice sighed and blurted out, "But his dad went to Stanford."

> **No, your child will not just "snap out of it."**

It can be tempting to think that because you or your spouse went to a top school, did very well at any school, or became successful later in life, there is no way you could have a child who can't read, write, or focus. Here's what you need to know: There's nothing wrong with your child's IQ. They may just be wired differently than you but are probably every bit as smart. Your child has a different way of learning. Thinking back, maybe you, or someone in your family, had that same learning style. Research shows that learning differences can run in families.

"He loves to be read to," Alice went on. "And he loves roller coasters, LEGO, Pokémon, *Star Wars*, and building."

"As long as he has passions," I told her, "I will be able to teach him to read and write. When can we meet?"

"I'll talk to my husband," Alice told me, "and call you back."

TWO YEARS LATER

Two years passed before I finally got another call from Alice. "When I told my husband about you, he said Jack didn't need help. He told me he'd been just like Jack when he was younger, and he turned out fine."

This was a classic case of "He'll snap out of it."

But Alice was calling again because Jack was in third grade, and he was really struggling.

When Jack arrived at my house a few weeks later, he jumped from the entryway platform directly onto the back of my white couch. Then he tumbled on the cushions and careened to the carpet below. All the while he'd somehow kept his shoes off the couch.

"Jack," his mom yelled, "Vicki doesn't want your dirty shoes on her couch."

"My feet are in the air, and I haven't touched her couch. By the way, Vicki, what were you thinking when you bought all white furniture?"

"Jack, I have no idea. I never thought every student would enter my house and jump from the platform directly onto my white couch. Never crossed my mind."

"Big mistake." He maneuvered off the floor, still being considerate not to let his shoes touch the couch. "Hey, look what I brought," he said.

Alice looked exhausted. She collapsed on the nearest chair and dropped a large bag on the floor.

"I brought my ball python to show you." Jack opened the drawstring on his mother's Gucci bag. What emerged astonished me, and I screamed.

"Ugh," I tried to get as far away from the 3-foot python as I could. "A snake. What do you feed him? People?"

Jack sat down cross-legged as his mom carefully wrapped it around his body. "Rats," he answered.

"Where do you get rats?"

"For God's sake, Vicki, not at the farmers' market on Sunday. At a pet store. They come frozen. My dad uses tweezers to pick up the frozen rat, and I put it in the snake's mouth." Jack put the snake back in the bag and like a tornado went through the living room touching every object, book, piece of art, and pillow he saw. He followed me into the room where I teach and, even before sitting down, touched pencils, pictures, my computer, the drinking glass, and more.

A LATE START

Jack was extremely smart, but he came to me about two years later than he probably should have. By the time he got to my house, he had little confidence and all those years of not getting the attention he needed had resulted in his acting out, feeling impatient, and exhibiting oppositional/defiant behavior. He was now on the verge of getting kicked out of school.

Jack's father stopped believing he would "snap out of it" and allowed Jack to be tested by a neuropsychologist. Only then did Jack begin to get what he needed out of his education. That road would have been far less difficult for Jack and his family if they had intervened earlier. All the negativity and behaviors he'd accumulated over the past years being misunderstood had to be addressed before he would be ready to learn. It was a much longer process than it had to be.

"I'VE NEVER HEARD THAT STORY"

Often one parent thinks their child is the only one in the family to ever have learning differences or need extra help moving through school. I'd been seeing Mike, a first grader, for a few weeks when his mother told me no one in the family had any similar issues. But when I sat down with the man she'd been married to for 15 years, he said, "Oh, I was exactly like Mike. I could never read or write. Finally, in junior high I taught myself to read. I was really smart, but I just wasn't interested in school. Now I run three huge companies all over the world. I made it with no therapies."

His wife was looking at him like she'd never seen him before. "I've never heard that story," she told both of us.

Mike's dad just shrugged his shoulders.

The trouble was that their son needed more than Mike's father had. He wanted to learn to read and write, and because this was hard for him, he had no confidence and was acting out in class. The father's inability to see that his son did not want to wait until junior high to teach himself to read and write was problematic.

It took months, but dad finally realized Mike needed help.

When I worked with Sam, a second grader, and his grandmother dropped him off one day because his parents were out of town, she said, "Sam is exactly like his dad." Which was funny because when I'd met the parents, I'd asked if either had any issues in school, and they'd both said no. "His dad was tutored all through school," she told me.

DENIAL IS A POWERFUL FORCE

During the 30 years I worked in Los Angeles as a reading teacher, I would have parent-teacher conferences twice a year with the parents of the children who came to me for a pull-out reading class. When I tried talking to one mom and dad about a speech evaluation for their child's tongue thrust and lisp, they looked at me like I was crazy. "You must be thinking of another child." The mother shook her head. "Not our six-year-old," the father told me. The parents were so used to the way the child talked, they never thought anything of his speech.

These instances happen not because the parents don't want to get help, but because as parents, we just get used to the way our child talks, acts, or learns. And, as mentioned, sometimes parents think their child will "snap out of it."

Teachers have a different set of problems when it comes to a child with learning differences. They may see a smart child who doesn't produce, and they think, wrongly, that the child is lazy. Laziness is a word often used to describe children. Take a hard look at your child: a learning difference or difficulty focusing might present as laziness, but that so-called laziness is just another red flag that tells us it is time for an intervention.

As soon as a professional sees a child isn't hitting growth milestones, they provide suggestions for early interventions. Maybe the teacher tells you that your child can't focus in class or is having trouble climbing the play structures. Maybe there's a red flag around speech, hearing, eyesight, or physical activities. You might hope your child will grow out of these, but it is always wise to get an opinion from a professional. If you have any questions about your child, start with your pediatrician. As a nation, we've grown a lot in 10 years. A decade ago, if you noticed your child was not hitting certain growth milestones or was different from other children, your pediatrician might have said, "Don't worry, your child is fine. Kids progress at their own rate."

Today, if you're noticing early issues like not walking, talking, crawling, listening, or thinking, keep in mind that every state provides intervention services under the Individuals with Disabilities Education Act (IDEA). These services may be free or at a low cost.

If you notice some delays later, start again with your doctor and then seek other professionals based on your child's needs. There are regional centers in many states. Regional centers diagnose children with developmental disabilities and delays. You can take your child there from birth to three years old. The regional center will determine if your child qualifies for services to help them with their special needs. The center will inform, educate, and support you in this process and are inexpensive when compared to individual therapists. You can also check your health insurance. Many therapies for children are covered under insurance plans.

> When I meet a parent for the first time there are a few questions I always ask:
>
> - Was it a normal pregnancy? Was the child early? Were there any difficulties?
>
> - Did your child meet the normal milestones for crawling, walking, other physical activities, and talking?
>
> - How does your child get along with other children or siblings?
>
> - Does your child have any eating, dressing, or sleeping issues?

- Does your child have any emotional issues?

- Has your child had an eye exam by a pediatric ophthalmologist who checks for seeing close-up, such as letters on a page, rather than just focusing on the distance exam like the one in the doctor's office?

- Has your child had a hearing test? Your child needs to hear the sounds of a word correctly to decode and spell. The child has to hear the teacher give directions.

- Has your child had a speech and language evaluation by a speech and language pathologist?

- Has your child seen an occupational therapist for writing or any other difficulties?

- Does your child have difficulty focusing?

These questions give you a sense of what to look for in your child.

THE TAKEAWAY

Remember that a gut feeling is always one of the best indicators. You often can't rely on the mind alone—it can play tricks of denial—or you may simply know your child so well that you missed something. Pay close attention to everything about your child and just as you do with the gut feeling, listen to your doctor, the teachers, or even friends and family. And, most important, investigate early.

[3]

A Guide Through
the Testing Process

Patrick Dempsey, star of *Grey's Anatomy*, was tested as a 12-year-old and found to have learning differences. Before that he was misdiagnosed and put in special-education classes. Getting the right testing made all the difference.

———————— // ————————

Many parents have come to me asking what is wrong with their child. I find what is "right" with their child and try to guide the parents through the testing process that I think should be given to their child.

This past year I was working with Mason, a very bright first grader who was having difficulty with reading and writing and had speech issues. The biggest challenge was his lack of focus.

Rather than make him feel like a failure by having him focus on what didn't interest him, I kept him focused on his passions and abilities rather than his differences. Mason loved animals and knew facts about every animal I mentioned. He couldn't remember many of the high-frequency words that make up 50% of every page in every book—"the," "this," "what," "that"—but he never forgot that "tiger" had the long-vowel sound of *i*.

YOU:
"What's wrong with my child's brain?"

ME:
"What's *right* with your child's brain?"

Every week, I communicated with Mason's teacher to make sure I was focusing on the same skills she was. I call this "double-dose teaching." He was progressing academically, but he was still being challenged in class with severe inattention that greatly impacted his learning. Halfway through the year his mother, Marla, was called into the principal's office for a discussion.

Imagine being a child in elementary school being called into the principal's office—the worry and fear, the feeling that you might throw up. What's going to happen?

Triple that feeling being a parent who is well aware her child is struggling. When Marla was called in, she was nervous. She became even more anxious when the principal told her that Mason needed to be tested by a neuropsychologist. The testing, Marla was told, would be a good way to understand the best approach to teaching him. Marla came away with the names of three neuropsychologists.

That afternoon, when I opened my front door, Marla was standing there alone looking as though someone had just died. She didn't have to tell me what had happened. I had observed the same shocked, sad faces after many parents had visited the principal's office. I knew she was about to ask me, in her quivering voice, what every parent asks: "What's wrong with my child's brain?"

Though all my parents have that gut feeling about their child, they still hope that with help from the reading specialist, their bright child will simply "snap out of it!" And when that doesn't happen, intense parental anxiety occurs—coupled with the fact that the testing process is daunting.

DEMYSTIFYING THE TESTING PROCESS

Let's go through the process.

Most principals will start by giving you the names of private professionals who do the testing to determine your child's strengths and weaknesses, both educationally and emotionally. They may also suggest you use your local school district to get the testing done. You can get your child tested privately or publicly or both.

Every professional who tests your child will give you a lot of paperwork to fill out. The background information forms are important: pregnancy, birth, early years, sleep patterns, siblings, and family backgrounds. Try to be exact. If your child is receiving any other therapies, like speech or occupational therapy, make sure you add this information to the forms.

The behavior form is equally valuable. It is given to parents, teachers, and any other professionals your child might be seeing. Again, be completely honest. This checklist is incredibly important. The person testing your child can get vital information from these questionnaires. A lot of what the tester uses in the evaluation comes from parents, teachers, and therapists. So, make sure everyone gets a form and sends it in before the testing begins.

PRIVATE TESTING

One thing to remember is that public schools will not look at private school tests. If you are in a public school, it will only accept its own IEP (Individualized Education Program) testing, not any outside testing you did.

Your principal, or the school's learning specialist, will have a list of professionals who can evaluate your child privately. They should know the credentials of the people on this list and be able to tell you why they chose those specific professionals for you to call. You might also call your child's pediatrician to get some names.

Private evaluators fall under a few categories that have to do with level of education and exactly what they are testing.

Neuropsychologists are professionals with PhDs who specialize in brain processing and functioning. They provide the most thorough test. It is best to check with your insurance company to see if they will cover the test because it can be expensive. The neuropsychologist's entire process takes several hours over several days. Their test is the most comprehensive because they usually have the latest research on learning differences and are familiar with how learning relates to brain function.

Neuropsychologists will tell you what your child's strengths and weaknesses are because they have administered many tests. They are not medical doctors who will write prescriptions. They are not educators who will teach your child. They usually don't offer comprehensive educational suggestions. As one mom lamented to me, after going to the meeting with the neuropsychologist for the test results, "It was 60 pages long and to understand what the doctor was telling me I needed a dictionary."

Clinical psychologists also have a PhD and license and can do a complete psycho/educational assessment of intellectual and emotional functioning. They also do therapy for emotional and behavior problems. They cannot prescribe medication.

Developmental pediatricians (DPs) are medical doctors who mostly test children five years or older (although they do sometimes test younger children) to evaluate which developmental milestones they have achieved.

You might go to a DP early on when you have that gut feeling that something is wrong with your child. DPs administer shorter tests, so they take less time. Considering that younger children have inconsistent stamina, attention, and cooperation, the shorter time may be advantageous.

The tests DPs administer include cognitive tests, achievement tests, and fine motor tests. If your child has any attention differences and needs meds, a DP can help you. They will also follow your child longitudinally so they have more insight into how your child does over time and if certain interventions are helping or not.

Once you get their names, call the professionals. Ask some questions on the phone to get a feeling if the professional would be a good fit for your child.

- What is the procedure?

- What tests are given?

- When are the tests given?

- How many days will it take?

- What are your credentials?

- How long have you been doing testing?

PUBLIC SCHOOL TESTING

Public schools give IEP tests for free, unlike the private tests that can cost a lot of money. You can get your child tested in the public school in the area you live in. This test is given by a trained learning professional who will evaluate your child's present levels of academic achievement.

If you choose to go the public school route, then you may not choose your evaluator for this test. The professionals in your public school who handle testing will assign you a professional in your district who will test your child. This test is shared with your school and follows your child through all their years of school. If you get a private test for your child, you do not have to share the results with your public school.

PREPPING THE TESTER TO MEET YOUR CHILD

Make sure to tell the person testing your child what your child's passions and strengths are. Your child will spend several hours over several days with this person, so if you give them some personal information ahead of time, it might make the testing less stressful for your child. I told one doctor that my student loved LEGO bricks, so she had them at the testing to let him build something before she started testing him.

In my own practice when I test a child's reading ability, I always ask the parent what the child likes. It can be a TV show, a LEGO set, a football team, or Pokémon. Then I am ready with information or some items related to what they like. The child usually comes in a bit afraid of meeting someone new who is going to test them and find out they can't read. Being ready with something they like, and can talk about, not only lessens stress but gives me great insight into the child that can't be found on a reading test.

After you have completed and sent in the behavior forms and background information, your child will go through a battery of tests. I am quite impressed with the testing students receive now. It has improved tremendously in the last several years.

Public or private, the evaluator assesses many aspects about your child, including speech, language, behavior, and attention. There are intelligence tests, processing speed tests, and academic achievement tests, including phonological awareness, writing, math, and language (receptive and expressive) tests. There are also fine and gross motor development, attention and concentration, learning and memory, and social and emotional functioning tests.

TESTING WITH AND WITHOUT MEDICATION

A child with difficulty focusing may not perform as well on tests without medication. Most private evaluators will tell you to start the attention medication *after* being tested and then come back in six months to be retested on medication. The medication could change the test scores significantly. The problem is, because the test is expensive, if the child is doing well in school *on* medication, the parents often won't go back for retesting. But I've seen intelligence scores go from very low off medication to much higher six months later when the child is on medication.

If you want to know your child's true intelligence scores, try to go back for a second testing when the medication seems to be working.

There are other problems with testing that don't involve medication. When I was teaching in an elementary school in Los Angeles, I taught Ben in my pull-out reading center. An engaging, creative fourth grader, he was having trouble with learning, attention, and his emotions. I had seen a contest for kids on the internet asking them to build something and then write a story about it. Ben entered the contest, using LEGO bricks, which he loved, and built the most fantastic boat. He then wrote a story about kids living on the boat, getting to do anything they wanted because no parents were allowed on it.

Ben won the contest. His winning story was posted on the contest site, with a picture of his boat. His confidence soared.

QUESTIONING UNEXPECTED RESULTS

But then a newly licensed neuropsychologist was asked to test Ben, and she concluded that he was a nonreader. I was stunned. After two years, he had become a proficient reader with great comprehension. Writing was still difficult for him, and he still exhibited inattention and a lot of emotionality, but he *was* reading. In my reading room I asked him, "What happened during that testing with Dr. Deborah? I know you can read."

"There was a *Ski Aspen* poster in her room," Ben answered, "and my dad has cancer and I was wondering if we'd be going skiing this winter if he was still so sick. I just couldn't pay attention to anything she said."

Sadly, Ben's 38-year-old dad died before ski season that year.

In my opinion the test score did not show Ben's true ability. He had not been paying attention at all that day.

When I told Dr. Deborah that he was actually a strong reader, she was surprised. I brought her into my classroom to hear Ben read. After listening to Ben read and then answer all the comprehension questions correctly, she said to me, "How did you know Ben was such a strong reader?"

"Experience and interaction with a child. That's how I know," I told her.

Testing can show only one part of a child's abilities and differences. Ben was thinking about his sick dad, not about reading. The best information a professional can gain about a child before testing begins is from the parents, teachers, and therapists.

PREPARING YOUR CHILD FOR TESTING

Before being tested, Jeff, one of my third graders, said, "I was so scared when I went to Dr. Jayne. My parents had been

27

fighting and were freaked there was something wrong with my brain. I thought there was something wrong or else I'd be reading, and I couldn't."

Jeff was smart but unable to read or write at more than a first-grade level. One detriment to his learning was his lack of attention. I had referred the family to Dr. Jayne, a neuro-psychologist. She would be evaluating Jeff. Though Jeff was nervous, the results of this testing helped his family get the right support for him.

With the cooperation of Jeff's parents, I began educational therapy with him, and he was put on medication for his inattention. The medication helped Jeff concentrate in class and access all he knew because he was so smart. Though he'd been anxious about the testing, he was greatly helped by having done it.

Prepare your child for the tests. If you think *your* anxiety level is elevated, imagine your child's.

- Don't talk about the testing at home with your partner in front of the child or the other siblings.

- When you do talk about it, play up what they are good at, rather than focusing on what they can't do.

- Explain how the results of the testing will enable the teachers to give them more support at school.

- Make sure your child goes to bed on time the night before, and there is a good breakfast and plenty of time so you don't rush in the morning.

> • Ask if you can pack snacks for your child in case there is a break during testing. Pack protein over cookies. Make sure your child's teacher is aware that your child will be out of school and why.

AFTER THE TEST

After testing, do something fun and just hang out together. Don't pressure your child to talk about the testing.

The professional who tested your child will schedule a meeting with you to explain the results of the tests. The narrative of the report is usually many pages long and filled with terms you might not be familiar with. Unfortunately, as one neuropsychologist who tested a student said to me, "I am a neuropsychologist, not a teacher. I can only give you results of the tests. I can't tell you how to teach the child." The parents and the student's team have to find the right professionals to teach the child with a method that will work. If medication is needed, then you must go to a psychiatrist for a prescription.

You do not have to share the results of the private testing with school professionals. But discussing the test with school professionals can help you understand the results and how your child can be helped at school.

If you decide to tell your school about the test, a meeting at your child's school might include you, the tester, the principal, your child's teacher, the school specialist if there is one, and your child's educational specialist if you have one (see chapter 5 to learn about this important team member). The meeting is usually run by the principal or the learning specialist at the school.

MAKE THE MOST OF A MEETING

Your child's team can make all the difference between success and frustration, so don't hesitate to speak up if anything seems off. In general, everyone is doing their best, but every so often their best isn't sufficient.

The worst meeting I ever attended was in a school conference room with the parents, two outside psychologists, two teachers, the school psychologist, the principal, and me. The parents hadn't seen the report before they arrived at the meeting, which is unusual. It was 50 pages long! They were all stunned by the length. I had received the report three days before the meeting, and it had taken me, a professional, many hours to read and understand it. The neuropsychologist, who had done the testing, was brilliant and young, but she had no idea how to explain the results to the parents. She also did not know how to help the teachers teach the student. I tell this story not to alarm you but to give an extreme example of how well-meaning professionals can still miss the mark.

All too often, teachers aren't really prepared to teach children who learn differently. They may have read one chapter in a book on how to teach reading or had one class in college, but most have no real idea of how to support students with learning differences in the classroom. An action plan is sorely lacking from the reports. Teachers have children with learning differences in their classes and no direction on how to teach them. There needs to be more in-service for teachers. Until then, here are some suggestions for teachers on how to help a child with learning differences succeed:

- The student should be sitting as close as possible to the front of the room.

- The teacher should repeat directions to the student.

- The student should be given extra time on tests.

- The teacher should communicate with the educational specialist who is trained to work with students with learning differences.

- If the student is on medication, the teacher should be aware of any change in the child's behavior and notify the parent of the changes.

THE TAKEAWAY

The testing process can seem scary and daunting, but in fact it can be the first step toward success for your child. Think of these tests not as the kind that you pass or fail but rather as a diagnostic tool that will help your child get the support they need to thrive.

Depending on the results of the test, a referral to a speech/language pathologist, occupational therapist, or psychologist may be in order. But the most important action you can take after testing is to hire the best educational specialist you can. Chapter 5 will tell you everything you need to know about them, but in short a good educational specialist will be able to understand the test results and how to work with your child using their strengths and passions.

Over and over I hear from my students about the specialists who helped them on their journey. They will often tell me, "That relationship was the most important one of my career as a student." If you've gotten the best testing, now get the best educational specialist, a trained professional in learning differences who can explain the findings of the testing to you, relates well to your child, and will attend all meetings about your child's education.

[4]

Understanding ADHD and Getting Past the Fear of Medication

"Having ADHD and taking medicine for it is nothing to be ashamed of," says American gymnast Simone Biles, who has won a total of 32 Olympic and world championship medals, including 4 gold medals. This is a hard fact for many parents to hear, but understanding the difference medicine can make can be a game changer.

———————— // ————————

Many parents are afraid of giving their child medication to help them focus in school. This chapter will show how much medication can help your child who has learning differences.

If you have to call your child's name several times to get their attention, if your child daydreams a lot, if you have to tell your child something a few times in order for them to understand, your child may be labeled ADHD/Inattentive, the standard that doctors, mental health professionals, and clinicians use when they're assessing and diagnosing ADHD and other mental health issues as per the American Psychiatric Association's *Diagnostic and Statistical Manual of Mental Disorders.*

UNDERSTANDING ADHD

In 1987 ADD (attention deficit disorder) was revised to ADHD (attention deficit hyperactivity disorder) because professionals who wrote the manual felt that hyperactivity was an important characteristic of ADD. The child I described in chapter 1, who ran around the perimeter of his yard and wouldn't stop, had ADHD.

In 2013 the manual updated the definition of ADHD again to now include these three definitions. A child can be diagnosed with ADHD if they have one of the following presentations:

- ADHD, combined presentation, in which a child is inattentive and hyperactive.

- ADHD, predominantly inattentive presentation, in which the child is not hyper, just inattentive.

- ADHD, predominantly hyperactive-impulsive presentation, in which the child has impulsive behaviors and is hyperactive.

More information exists now on attention issues then in the 1970s and '80s. A lot of research has been done on students who exhibit the hyperactive aspect of attention as well as students who exhibit the inattentive aspect. The inattentive is harder to diagnose because these students aren't running all over the place, they just aren't paying attention or are lost in thought. But both hyperactive and inattentive mean that the student is not focusing on the work at hand, is not able to switch to different subjects during class time, or has a tough time completing assignments that take many steps.

Some hyperactive children may have difficulty with impulsive behavior, calling out in the classroom and being unable to contain their emotions. The child may not be able to listen or keep their hands off classmates.

The Centers for Disease Control and Prevention (CDC) has a list of symptoms of inattention and hyperactivity/impulsivity.

Inattention:

- Often doesn't give close attention to details or makes careless mistakes in schoolwork or other activities.

- Often has trouble keeping attention on tasks.

- Often does not listen when spoken to directly.

- Often does not follow through on instructions and fails to finish homework, chores, or duties (loses focus, gets sidetracked).

- Often has trouble organizing activities.

- Often doesn't want to do activities that take a lot of mental effort for a long period like homework.

- Often loses things.

- Often forgetful in daily activities.

Hyperactivity/Impulsivity:

- Often fidgets with hands or feet, squirms in seat.

- Often gets up from seat when supposed to remain there.

- Often runs about or climbs where not appropriate.

- Often has trouble playing or doing activities quietly.

- Is often on the go like a motor.

- Often talks excessively.

- Often blurts out answers.

- Often has trouble waiting for their turn.

- Often interrupts or intrudes on others (conversations or games).

If your child has been tested and found to have these kinds of attention issues, medication may or may not be needed. That is why having a psychiatrist on the team is of utmost importance.

Many factors influence how a child learns. When I met Trevor, he was in first grade, could not read, and had difficulty with physically writing and getting his thoughts on paper. He was very disorganized and inattentive in class.

Trevor spent a great part of the day looking out the window or fussing with things in his desk, not paying attention. Therefore, he was behind in academics. He was tested by a developmental pediatrician and found to have learning differences and attention deficit. One suggestion from the pediatrician was to hire an educational specialist to work with Trevor on reading and writing. I was called. Trevor was oppositional and not easy to teach, but I discovered he loved sharks. That was easy for me. I am a shark lover with a knowledge of sharks. I have a friend who is a shark expert. I used Trevor's shark passion to teach him the skills he needed to read and write.

THE RIGHT LEARNING ENVIRONMENT

Trevor's school was very structured with large classes and no tolerance for a child with learning differences. Trevor's parents looked elsewhere and finally found a school with smaller classes and teachers able to help students with learning differences and attention deficit. Trevor is now succeeding academically and never needed medication for his attention because he was more attentive in the new school with teachers who understood his educational needs.

I spoke with his mother to see how Trevor, now in fifth grade, was doing and she replied, "You know, because you made the sessions project-based and focused on sharks, he was interested and loved learning. To this day he can recite every fact about sharks you ever taught him."

Parents often wonder why their child is diagnosed with ADHD if they're not hyperactive. If you look closely at the testing report, you'll see that the word "inattentive" is usually added to the diagnosis: attention deficit hyperactivity disorder/inattentive. But the parents do not believe that their child has ADHD because they are able to focus for hours playing video games, watching sports, building, or even cooking. Alex, my seven-year-old student and expert chef with learning differences and ADHD/Inattentive, could always focus when I read stories with food as the topic (Tomie dePaola's *Pancakes for Breakfast*) and was focused when he went into the kitchen and cooked. In fact, he organized an entire YouTube video by preparing Nutella banana pizza and even wrote the recipe on a big poster board for the audience to see.

How can my child have ADHD when they're not hyperactive?

At home, if your child is working on something they love to do, they will be able to focus for hours and successfully complete the activity because the activity is something they are good at. They aren't trying to do something that is hard for them. In other words, your child may not be able to listen in school or complete homework, but they can still build with LEGO bricks for hours.

One of my students, Max, had severe ADHD. He lacked attention and was very defiant and argumentative. His parents had him tested and the doctor felt medication would greatly help him, but the parents refused to put him on medication. One day he brought in pictures of his dining room at home. His mom had cleared out the entire huge dining room of all furniture, and he had built a massive LEGO city: buildings, parks, houses, larger than any I had ever seen. "I let him do it any time he wants. Then he doesn't get into trouble or argue with me. He works almost every day on this project."

BUILD ON YOUR CHILD'S INTERESTS

I used LEGO bricks when I taught Max to engage him and keep him focused. He would build something, then he had to write a story using the LEGO object in the story. In my experience most of my students are above average in intelligence, but more than anything else, they have passions. I use their interests and abilities to teach them to read and write because I know they'll focus if the activities are built around their interests.

In many of my classes the inattentive students look out the window, fidget with a pencil, or stare into space, not listening. Melissa, a second grader I worked with in my study, was staring out the window.

"What are you thinking about?" I knew she had not been paying attention to anything I said.

"Oh," she told me. "Do you know there is a huge alligator in your tree right here outside your window?" She'd apparently been looking at it for two years. "Do you see it?"

The window in my study is similar to Frank Lloyd Wright's house at Fallingwater, where the living room window overlooks the middle of a tree so you feel like you're in the sky. I never noticed that the bark looked like an alligator, but now whenever I look out the window, I see the alligator, and I'm reminded of Melissa.

Melissa is ADHD/Inattentive. She is not hyperactive. She is just quietly not paying attention and cannot focus on what I am teaching or listen to the teacher in class. She is thinking her own thoughts.

Harry, a second grader with ADHD/Inattentive, described his brain to me: "Dr. Waller, every second of every day my brain is thinking. Thousands of thoughts go through my head in a day. I never listen in class or call out. I'm in my own world." It was heartbreaking to hear how difficult school was for this creative, smart boy with severe ADHD. Unfortunately, his parents would not get him tested or get him help.

WHY SOME CHILDREN CAN'T FOCUS

Children with ADHD or ADHD/Inattentive will not focus when they're in school because the work is too hard and they have to expend too much energy to listen and complete the work. Their inability to focus on subjects they're not interested in prevents them from doing the academic activities required in class. When that same child is learning about their passion, like sharks, they may be able to pay attention but still may not be able to read or write about sharks. If asked about the subject they are interested in, these students can tell you, verbally, everything about the subject, and so some parents think that they will be fine without medication.

I remember when Paul, a third grader, who had incredible, creative story ideas, was tested and found to have attention issues and his father told me, "I think he can manage without meds. I was tested for ADHD, and I've made 20 million dollars. I never took medication. He doesn't need it." Many years later, I ran into his mother at the grocery store, and she told me her son had gone through many therapists throughout high school. None of them worked. They all said he needed medication. But his father wouldn't allow it. As a result, Paul never finished school. He went from job to job. I wonder if he ever found happiness.

One of the most distressing stories about children and medication happened late one night. The phone rang. It was the mother of one of my students. She said she'd been arguing with her husband about putting their son, Corey, on medication. They'd had him tested, and he had ADHD, learning differences, and a high IQ. The doctor thought the meds would calm him down and help him to focus so he could learn. Corey's dad refused to put him on medication. This particular night Corey had been trying to do his homework, and the mom heard her husband and Corey screaming at each other. Corey wouldn't do his homework and John had sent him upstairs to bed, homework unfinished. The mom went to talk to her husband, but he was very upset.

When the parents finally went upstairs, they found Corey asleep in their bed. There was the worst smell in the room, and their bare feet squished into the wet, soggy carpet. Corey had opened a bottle of the mom's perfume and poured it all over the bedroom carpet. The mom begged me to call the dad to convince him to let Corey try medication for his ADHD. I wasn't sure if this was the best time to have a heart-to-heart with Dad. But I called him.

And sure enough, when Dad got on the phone he was very defensive. "This is insane," he said. "I think Corey is lazy and doesn't try and now look what he did. We can't even sleep in our own room."

"Listen," I said, "you had Corey tested by a good neuropsychologist. Corey is smart, not lazy, but has learning differences and ADHD. What you experienced tonight was his frustration in not being able to concentrate and do his homework, so he lashed out at you. The doctor recommended meds. Why are you so opposed to letting Corey try them?"

Dad said he'd been just like Corey as a kid, and he turned out to be very successful, so why should he put his child on meds. "Let him tough it out."

I tried to explain that Corey was not him. "He needs meds. Maybe you never did."

THE MORE YOU KNOW

Months later, Corey was on medication, seeing me for educational therapy, and had started succeeding in school. Dad, a successful businessman, decided to get an evaluation, too. He dealt with many of the same issues as Corey. He was frustrated with Corey because he saw himself in his son. The dad was tested and found to have ADHD and learning differences, too.

When he started to take meds, he called me. "I can't believe how much better I feel," he said. "I get so much work done now that I'm on medication. And with Corey on meds, too, dinnertime is great."

Statistics on ADHD:

- ADHD is inherited. Over 30% of students with ADHD have at least one parent with ADHD, and if both parents have it, the risk is one in three a child will have it.

- Medication helps four out of five of these cases.

- The medication that is prescribed for a child should be monitored constantly to see which medication is best, how much is given, and whether it's generic or brand.

Many professionals don't tell parents that the child needs medication because they are worried the parents will get upset. My student, Alex, had been getting therapies for years: occupational therapy, speech, and even reading. No one ever mentioned his inattention, which was his biggest challenge and impacted all his learning. When I asked his reading tutor why she never said anything, she answered, "It's not my place." She didn't want to rock the boat. Well, then whose place is it?

Medication can be a very scary decision for parents. A tremendous amount of misinformation exists out there, and it can make you feel out of control and anxious. After your child has been tested and diagnosed with attention difficulties, the professional evaluator will give you names of psychiatrists who prescribe medication.

The "team" meeting a few times a year, with all the professionals working with your child, ensures that all bases are covered. The psychiatrist answers any questions the teachers and therapists ask and discusses whether there might be any changes in the child's behaviors. The medication might not be the correct one, or the dose is too much or too little. Sometimes the generic brand of medicine doesn't work, but the "brand" medicine does work.

> If your child is on medication, note that:
>
> • Any person working with your child has to be aware of and report any change in behavior. A psychiatrist will be seeing your child frequently to see if the meds are working.
>
> • Teachers, who see your child daily, may notice changing behaviors and think it's just the child's attention issues.
>
> • Educational specialists or other therapists might notice changing behaviors in your child but, again, not know what they should be looking for.

UNDERSTAND YOUR MEDICATION OPTIONS

If your child needs medication, there are options that have to be considered. Some medications calm the student down, some help with focusing. I am not a medical doctor, so what follows is a short summary of the types of medication given to children who are diagnosed with attention differences.

There are two types of ADHD medications: stimulants and non-stimulants. These medications can help your child focus in class, remember more of what they read and hear, and become calmer. From my personal observations, when students are given the proper medication, they are able to access what I teach and use it.

Stimulants can be taken in different doses. They can be taken two or three times a day or once a day if a longer acting one. The methylphenidate type and amphetamine type have shorter and longer-acting formulas. Non-stimulant medications are not as strong but may be milder in terms of side effects. These might take weeks to show the best result. Your doctor will give you much more detailed information about these medications, what to look for, side effects, and which medication will be the best for your child.

Children who are normally on medication but for whatever reason are no longer on it may come to an unknown word and skim over it. Or they may say an incorrect word and keep reading. It isn't that they haven't been taught the word or don't know how to decode it; it's that they lack the focus to stop and decode it. This creates challenges in reading comprehension. One of my students described his brain when he was off medication as "a speeding train all day long. I can't stop how fast it's going, so I can't do my work or concentrate at all."

MONITORING YOUR CHILD'S MEDS

This year I had a fifth grader, Gerry, who was on medication for his attention issues. I was in weekly contact by email with his parents, teachers, and psychiatrist. At first his grades were going up, but all of a sudden he began calling out in class, fighting with kids, and even impulsively yelling at teachers and the principal. I knew something was wrong. He'd been doing so well, and then all of the sudden his behavior changed. The teacher explained that his impulsive behavior was manifesting in the classroom. I thought the medication had to be adjusted and immediately called his mom and emailed his doctor. He had been on the same meds for three years and, after he saw his doctor, his meds were adjusted and he stopped acting out impulsively.

Another fifth grader, whose parents normally left his pill out for him to take, decided on his own to stop taking it. All of a sudden, his behavior in school and at therapy appointments changed. He was unfocused and hyper. Fortunately, the team was all in contact and communicated with each other about his behavior, which helped uncover the problem. Parents need to administer medication to their child, not give the child the responsibility. It can be dangerous to put meds in the hands of a child. They can take too many or none at all.

Within a month of seeing my student Alex, I mentioned medication in a team meeting. The school principal, the school learning specialist, and Alex's dads were not happy. But because I was being proactive, they listened to me. He was going into second grade not reading, was unable to form letters, and had speech problems and a variety of language problems, and I was pretty sure he was ADHD/Inattentive. He had no focus at all! The school principal was upset with me and warned that they don't tell parents to get their child tested until third grade. But by third grade, a child with learning differences and an inability to focus who can't read or write will lose confidence and be miserable. Why wait?

After Alex was tested and diagnosed with ADHD/Inattentive, he started taking medication and his focus improved dramatically. When I repeated something I had taught him off the meds, he could access it once he was on meds. "Vicki," he told me one day, "when I wasn't on medication, I could still hear what you were teaching in my brain, I just couldn't reach it. Now that I'm on meds, I remember everything you taught me and can use it!"

In the months after Alex got on medication and had undergone many hours of educational therapy, his reading soared. The subjects that still gave Alex—and many of my students—difficulty were physical writing (if they have occupational therapy issues), processing their thoughts and writing them down, and executive functioning issues like organizing, completing tasks, and keeping up effort to do what they are supposed to do. Some students have spelling issues, which also impact their writing.

One of my former students came to me in fifth grade. She'd been tested in second grade and told she had learning differences and was ADHD/Inattentive, but her parents hadn't put her on medication. Now she ran up and said, "Dr. Waller, I'm on meds now and I can focus in class! And I'm smart just like you said I was." It took her parents three years to finally accept the diagnosis and put her on medication as the professionals had suggested. Then she became a successful student and a happy person. Sara graduated from Brown a few years ago.

Elizabeth, whom I mentioned in chapter 1, was on medication but felt the classes at her high school were too big. It was difficult for her to get the individual help she needed. With her mom's help Elizabeth changed to a school with smaller classes and teachers who were willing to help her individually. She also worked with the same educational specialist for many years.

Elizabeth advocated for herself. When she was in college, she met with her teachers and told them about her issues and was often allowed to take tests orally. She took project-based classes because she did very well in those. She used planning as a tool to help her through. She planned out when to study for each class. When she had a test she would start studying a few weeks beforehand. She is still on medication for her attention issues and, as I said in chapter 1, is now a very successful stylist dressing Hollywood stars. She called me recently and started the conversation this way: "I thought about all the schools I went to, including college. I did well because I would never take no for an answer."

THE TAKEAWAY

From my experience, once children with attention issues are put on medication the learning becomes easier. Their learning differences and attention issues don't entirely go away, but they are able to access more of what they learn once they are on medication. The first step after your child is tested and diagnosed by a qualified professional is to see a psychiatrist who will monitor the medication. Another important part of the puzzle is for all professionals who work with your child to keep a close watch on the child's actions and moods while on medication and frequently report back to the "team."

[5]

How to Choose an
Educational Specialist
for Your Child

CNN news anchor Anderson Cooper was diagnosed with
learning differences as a child and is grateful to his reading specialists for the role they played in his career success.
They encouraged him to find books that he was passionate
about. These understanding teachers changed everything
for him. It made all the difference in his life early on.

———————————— // ————————————

After your child is tested, how do you decide who is going
to work with your child? When Trevor, a first grader, was

diagnosed with learning differences and ADHD/Inattentive, his mother, Marcia, inquired about getting help for him. The doctor gave her a list of names of educational specialists. Her friends gave her some names of tutors. Trevor's school principal gave her the names of some educational specialists and tutors, as well. She wound up interviewing 15 tutors and several educational specialists. Marcia found a big difference between tutors and educational specialists. Tutors either were very young with a college degree in education but no real training in how to teach a child with learning differences and ADHD, or were mature women who had taught but had no experience with children with learning differences.

BEWARE THE "QUICK FIX"

Because this process is unwieldy, parents can run from specialist to specialist or to a reading center looking for a "quick fix." Certain places will promise you: "We will have your child improve in reading by four years in just eight weeks." And the cost is $6,000. Jill took her son, Evan, to one of those "fix it" places that advertises magical reading growth. "He was going to learn in four weeks and we'd be done, but he cried every day because it was so boring and he was miserable. To this day he hates reading and is still struggling." When the claim turns out to be false, many parents run from "fix" to "fix" instead of looking for a trained educational specialist who can really help their child to succeed.

There is no magical or immediate cure. If you do the research and find a knowledgeable educational specialist or teacher who has training in teaching children with differences, they will go with you and your child on the journey to success and happiness.

You want an educational specialist or an educator with a doctorate in learning differences to work with your child. They have advanced degrees and have been trained past their college education to evaluate and work with children with learning differences. Whoever you choose should advocate for your child and develop good relationships with teachers and other professionals and work as part of a team. They should visit your child's class and work closely with the teacher. Otherwise, the teacher is asking you, the parent, to communicate with the specialist, and desired goals get lost in translation.

Sometimes I am the 15th call parents make. "The minute we spoke on the phone, and you asked me what my son's passions were," one mother said, "I knew you would be the one." Later she told me it didn't hurt that I had a doctorate in reading and learning differences and had taught for many years. At any rate, this chapter is designed to help you cut down the time it takes to find the right educational specialist for your child.

HOW TO CHOOSE AN EDUCATIONAL SPECIALIST

The following points should be included in your conversation with an educational professional:

Pick an educational specialist who is familiar with testing results. Ask about their experiences reading reports from professionals who have tested the child and how they use the report to teach your child. If they are trained, they will be able to do this. The report is very difficult for a layperson to understand without a professional discussing it with you.

You want a trained specialist who knows how to work with children with learning differences. Educational specialists must be trained with degrees in this area of expertise and have the tools, new techniques, and tips to work with your child. When you interview specialists for your child in any discipline, find out what degrees they have. A college degree in literature doesn't mean they know how to teach your child to read. Ask about their background, including their degrees and experience working with children with learning differences.

- What grade levels do they teach? I work with elementary students ages 4 to 12. If you need a middle-school specialist, you have to find one who specializes in that age group. Do they teach reading, writing, math?

- How often and for how long will they see the child? If someone tells you it will take exactly eight weeks, I'd be suspicious. One of my parents told me of a place she went to that "will teach your child to read in four weeks." When she interviewed the owner of the business, she was told they use college students whom they train in the methods they use. No one can give a time limit on how long it will take a child to learn to read and write—not even a specialist. One hour a week is usually not enough. It often has to be 1.5 hours and reading at home, too. It's impossible to know from the beginning how many weeks, months, or even years learning to read can take.

- Find out how they intend to motivate your child. What is their approach? Do they teach from passions, like baseball? What kinds of materials do they use? Ask to see them. Are they workbooks, games, or real reading material? I am a huge proponent of reading actual books. I helped a student who worked with an educational specialist for two years, and they never opened a book. She used lots of games and computer systems but no real books!

- Will the therapists you choose be part of the team and communicate with teachers and other therapists who work with your child? This is very important. There must be communication between the team members. Will therapists email teachers to find out what is expected of the child that week? Will they help with those lessons?

- Will they help with your child's homework? Will they give your child homework that you have to help with? Make sure it isn't too much, particularly if it's added to school homework. Your child doesn't need more anxiety. Reading every night or being read to is a good homework assignment from an educational specialist.

- Where is their office? Or do they come to your home? Location can be important, especially with after-school traffic.

- How much do they charge and what is their availability? Do they work weekends? Are they flexible if the child has a dance recital and you need to cancel or change an appointment? Do they charge for missed sessions? Most specialists will have a 24-hour cancellation notice. I have found it is difficult to charge for illness when working with children who can get sick at any time. Do they do school visits and do they charge for that? Many specialists will visit your child's class and attend a meeting about your child. Make sure you know if they charge.

- How often do they evaluate your child to check improvement? I know a student who was tutored for two years and never evaluated. After two years, she was failing in school and, when tested at her school, was still not reading. As a parent you can request an evaluation to see how your child is progressing.

Once you feel these questions have been answered sufficiently, make an appointment for you and your child to meet the specialist. I call this a meet-and-greet time. Be sure to ask if there is a charge for the meet and greet. In my own practice, I never charge for this session.

Prepare your child for the first meeting by suggesting they ask the specialist anything they want to know, though most children don't have anything to ask. But it's wise to give them this opportunity. At this session you will get a feel for the specialist's personality, how they engage your child, and the chemistry the two of them have. After you leave, talk with your child to see if they would want to spend extended time with this person. I've never found a parent and child who did not get a "feeling" about a specialist. But remember, do that phone call first. You know your child and what kind of person they might like.

THE TAKEAWAY

Be sure to connect with the right specialist for your child's needs, using the guidelines in this chapter.

Once you've hired an educational specialist, be consistent and try not to miss many sessions. It is very important for your child's progress. I had a child who missed 8 out of 10 sessions with me and the mom wondered why her child wasn't progressing. Also, stay on top of your child's learning. Give it time. The most important outcome, besides teaching your child, is the relationship the child has with the specialist. Both components are extremely important.

[6]

It Takes a Village

Cher, the multi-platinum recording artist, Broadway and movie star, and television personality, has said her report cards always stated she was not working up to her potential. Clearly, those teachers didn't have the tools to discover what her true potential could be!

———————————— // ————————————

When students with learning differences are interviewed about how they were able to succeed educationally and, later, in their adult lives, they often highlight the impact their parents, educational specialists, teachers, speech therapists, physical therapists, and others had on their success. Their parents and the professionals accepted their differences, provided them with access to content, and held them to high expectations. If a student had someone advocating on their behalf, it made all the difference in the world.

For 30 years, I worked in a school in Los Angeles as a reading specialist, helping children with learning differences. I had my own reading center and I saw up to 50 students a day.

Because of my education and experience in learning differences and children with attention issues, at meetings the principal held I tended to be the one telling parents to have the child tested, get the child assessed for speech and language issues, see about occupational therapy, or join a social group class if the child had social issues with other kids. I'd also connect with parents by phone to suggest ways to help their child at home.

> Building the right team can make all the difference in your child's success.

Many of the teachers I worked with didn't have experience teaching children who learned differently. So I would make suggestions on how to work best with students in the classroom, based on what I saw when they were in my reading center. Teachers would tell me what skills the child needed to work on, and I tailored the lessons in my room to integrate with their classroom curriculum. It became clear that in order for a child with learning differences to be successful, they had to have a support team.

Recently, I invited a speech pathologist, a physical therapist, an occupational therapist, and a pediatrician to discuss what factors would help a child with differences succeed. I was curious if what I had been finding for many years was similar to what other professionals found out about students with learning differences. Why did some succeed and others didn't? It was amazing. Five professionals came to the same conclusion: for a child who had learning differences to succeed, there had to be a team in place. A successful team includes the child's parents and all the professionals who work with their child.

YOUR FIRST TEAM MEETING

The first team meeting will probably be set up by your educational specialist, if you have one, or by the school's learning specialist. The meeting would include the professional who tested your child, so they can explain the testing results and answer any questions the team asks. Because they do not give any suggestions on how to teach your child—they only give test results—the meeting would also include the principal of the school, the child's teachers, and the learning specialist at the school, if there is one. Any other professional who works with your child, like an occupational therapist or a speech pathologist, would also attend. If you already have an educational specialist working with your child, they of course would attend. If you don't have your own specialist, at the meeting you can ask for a list of such specialists to interview who can work with your child.

WHAT IF YOUR TEAM BREAKS DOWN?

Unfortunately, a team approach can break down when one or more of the team refuses to cooperate. My student, Joey, was totally obsessed with soccer teams. I taught Joey to write stories using all the words associated with soccer: team, coach, goal, and so on. And I sent this information to his other therapists. The speech therapist used soccer words to help him with his speech. His occupational therapist used the soccer words to help him form letters and write. This was truly a fantastic team. Unfortunately, Joey's schoolteachers weren't interested in what we did with him, did not want suggestions from other professionals, and never gave his learning much attention. As a result, poor Joey hated school. It's very rare for a first grader to hate school. First grade is usually fun. Not for this child.

A child succeeds best working with an educational specialist *in combination* with the classroom teacher and parents. If there are exercises to do at home, definitely do them! I had two students from different families whose respective parents were taking them to a speech pathologist and were told they must practice every day. The five-minute exercises were short and could be done in the car on the way home from school. One set of parents was incredible and did the exercises every day. The other hardly did them, so the child really did exercises only with the speech therapist. The first child was finished in six months with his *r*'s and *l*'s. The other went on and off for two years.

Alex, the seven-year-old chef, had parents who kept a 300-page binder on their coffee table with over five years of reports about him from every therapist he had ever worked with. His school had required each therapist who worked with Alex and his team to do a write-up after every session, and these therapists were asked to email it to the teachers, principal, and parents. Part of my work with Alex, as his educational specialist, was continuing to keep all therapists in communication with each other, usually through email, but also through meetings twice a year with the whole team. We met to discuss lesson plans, what was working, his attention, and how Alex was succeeding.

THE TAKEAWAY

Now is all this easy? No. Do others want to take the time? Maybe not. Convincing other professionals with busy lives to keep in contact with all the professionals working with your child can be challenging and time-consuming. Choosing a great educational specialist can go a very long way. When they become your child's advocate, they also gather the team to work together. It is very advantageous for your child to have one person who will advocate for your child and put the team together. If you don't have an educational specialist, it may be the learning specialist at the school who initiates these meetings once or twice a year. But ideally all your child's therapists and teachers should work as a team with you.

To this day, I schedule school visits to my students' classes and keep in weekly email contact with their teachers, the professionals working with them, and their parents. I promote team meetings at the school and ask teachers to email me what will go on in class each week. The teacher may tell me they are studying oceans and words containing blends and digraphs, which gives me a chance to preteach, so that when the child goes into class, they know what the teacher is talking about. It gives them confidence. The success of a child with learning differences is aided by all the professionals you choose to work with your child. Choose wisely, choose the best, and don't give up.

[7]

The Importance of Teachers, Specialists, and Administrators in Your Child's Life

Pelé, regarded as the greatest soccer player of all time, had learning differences. He's been quoted as saying he believed that "success is no accident. It is hard work, perseverance, learning, studying, sacrifice, and most of all, love of what you are doing or learning to do."

—————————— // ——————————

After so many years of teaching students with learning differences, I understand what a huge impact teachers, specialists, and administrators have on the lives of children who learn differently. In my favorite book, *How Did You Get Here? Students with Disabilities and Their Journeys to Harvard,* by Thomas Hehir, many of the students interviewed said they got where they are because they had teachers who believed in them.

A few years ago, when Alex was in second grade, we had a team meeting at his school that included me, Alex's dads, his two classroom teachers, the principal, the school learning specialist, and his speech/language specialist. We waited for more than half an hour for the main teacher to appear. The principal had to call her three times. Finally, she walked in.

"I JUST DON'T KNOW HOW TO TEACH HIM"

When she sat down, she said, "I know you say how smart Alex is, but I just don't know how to teach him. I never had a kid like him."

We all knew how smart he was. I saw Alex four hours on Saturdays and three hours throughout the week. It was the most intensive work I had ever done with one of the most interesting, smartest, and kindest students I had ever known. The rest of his team were professionals who communicated with all of us every week, and they all saw Alex's unique brilliance.

Of course, this wasn't the first time a teacher was stumped as to how to teach a child like Alex, but this teacher looked completely uninterested.

As the year progressed, she never communicated with any of the team. When I went to observe Alex in class, I was stunned at what a horrific teacher she was. She had the students choose books for reading time and, while they read at their desks, she surfed the internet. She didn't engage in any directed teaching of reading with the children. Alex, a nonreader, often chose books that were too hard for him because she did not help the students choose their books. Then he sat there for an hour, pretending to read.

Luckily, she did not have her contract renewed at the end of the year, and the following year I saw a marked change in Alex. He had two great teachers who, although they admitted they really didn't know how to teach a student like Alex, were open to suggestions and communicated regularly with the team. These teachers saw how smart he was and noted how he learned best. He'd wanted to study Syria because he had a Syrian hamster, and his teacher agreed. In this way learning was more interesting. I learned more about the Syrian atrocities than I thought I'd ever want to know!

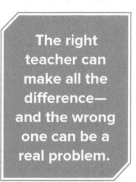

The right teacher can make all the difference—and the wrong one can be a real problem.

That same year I was the educational specialist for another student, Roger, a first grader who was working with a speech pathologist and an occupational therapist and was being tested for ADHD. He was very smart, but because of his attention issues, the teachers didn't recognize his intelligence. After Roger was put on medication for his ADHD, he was able to focus better in class. But that didn't mean his challenges disappeared. When I went for a school visit, I met his two seasoned teachers. Unfortunately, they had no idea how to help him and really weren't interested in anything he could do. They focused only on what he couldn't do. I visited that classroom often and watched his teachers give assignments without helping students who really needed it.

THE RIGHT TEACHER MAKES ALL THE DIFFERENCE

Roger's next year was amazing because his two teachers wanted to know how to help and were open to suggestions. They realized Roger had strengths. I worked with these teachers weekly. At one point, the teacher emailed me that Roger was dazed, not raising his hand, looking out the window, and then fighting with kids on the playground. This prompted me to contact his mom and have her take Roger to his psychiatrist to check his meds. It turned out he needed a larger dose of his medication.

Not every teacher has to work one-on-one with a student, but there is a way to teach independent work that doesn't leave students behind. I had a fourth grader, Danny, with a very structured teacher who rarely worked one-on-one. When I visited the class to see how she worked, she mostly gave directions, and the students followed what she said. She was teaching executive functioning, reporting, researching, and using outlines and directions. She wrote to me each week and told me what they were learning and what books they were reading so that I could read those books and help Danny with lessons and reports. Even though she wasn't creative or exciting, we were a great team. She was just what he needed and had a successful year.

Because US teacher-training programs at colleges do not have a lot of content on how to teach students who learn differently, it can be difficult for teachers to know how to teach them. The good teachers are willing to work with professionals to find ways to help. And schools are bringing in more training workshops for teachers on how to teach all students.

TOOLS FOR LEARNING

Many schools now have computers for students by third grade to make writing assignments easier. Keyboarding is a good way for students with processing, handwriting, and spelling differences to work more efficiently. Of course, keyboarding isn't everything. A child has to first get an idea, then access the sounds of words to be able to spell the words correctly or even spell-check. But at least if they learn to keyboard, they can process their thoughts faster and learn to spell-check.

Many teachers now require children to have assignment notebooks, so they can keep track of homework and upcoming tests. If you can, make sure you check that your child has it when they get home and remembers to take it back to school the next day.

WORKING WITH A CHALLENGING TEACHER

As a parent, it is frustrating when your child is in a class with a teacher they don't love. If this is the case, your child's educational specialist can often intervene and try to communicate with the teacher so that your child has a successful year. I have found that teachers listen to therapists more than they listen to parents. Even though not all teachers understand learning differences, if a therapist meets with them, they may become willing partners. Communication must be open and honest between all professionals.

Usually at the end of the report by the professional tester, there will be a few ideas for the teacher, too. The following are some ideas that you or your educational specialist can pass along to the teacher.

- Make sure the student has extra time to take a test if that is needed.

- Study pages for tests should be sent home and should also be sent to the educational specialist working with your student, with plenty of time for studying.

- It's best if the child can be seated close to you, the teacher, in case there are questions about assignments.

- After you give a direction, it's really helpful if you can stop by the child's seat and ask if they know what to do. Then ask the child to tell you what they are going to do.

- Children sometimes need extra time to answer when you ask a question. Alex told me he knows the answer, but with so many kids waving their hands and yelling out, he doesn't even try.

- Ask the teacher to post work online so that you and the educational specialist can look at what is nightly assigned or when reports are due.

IT'S NOT ALWAYS THE TEACHER

Sometimes it isn't the teacher who's the problem. Susan, a very smart kindergartner with learning differences and ADHD/Inattentive, was enrolled in a private school and had not been able to learn to read. The principal had a meeting with me, the child's reading specialist, her teacher, and the school counselor. After hearing what we all had to say, the principal set her file on the table. "Well." She sat back. "Susan will never get into our middle school. I think we should try to counsel her out."

I nearly fell off my seat. This was a very smart child who had challenges, but her parents were about to have her tested, I was assisting her in school daily, and she had a tutor outside school. She was only in kindergarten, and even with all this support, the principal was already saying Susan wouldn't get into seventh grade in seven years! How can anyone, especially the principal of a school, predict what will happen to a child in seven years? I was outraged.

Susan was tested, and she was diagnosed with learning differences and ADHD/Inattentive. The parents moved Susan to a smaller school with more individualized help and continued her outside educational therapy. She was a smart child and with good interventions was able to succeed in school. She became a drama teacher at a very good private school after college.

Eight years later, I was at a meeting for Wally, a second grader. Wally was an engaging student who knew every fact about weird sea creatures. I was helping him read and write after school. The principal looked at me during the meeting and said, "So, when will Wally be normal?"

I'd never heard anyone say this about a student. Luckily, Wally's parents took him out of that school and transferred him to a school where he had a good team of teachers and a great principal. We all worked together helping him succeed. He gained confidence and could access all that he learned. Wally is in sixth grade now, still talking about weird sea creatures and doing well.

THE TAKEAWAY

It is impossible for me to tell you what to do when you know the teacher is not the right fit for your child. Most schools will not change a child's class once they're in it. Instead of making your life and your child's life miserable, get the best therapists outside school for your child. The therapist you hire can advocate for your child. As an educational specialist, I find I can get more for my students by talking to the teachers myself than the parent can.

[8]

For the Love of Reading

Albert Einstein, who had learning differences, stated, "Most teachers waste their time by asking questions that are intended to discover what a pupil does not know, whereas the true art of questioning is to discover what the pupil does know or is capable of knowing."

———————— // ————————

I had a principal say to me, "All you do is make kids love to read."

And I replied, "If that's all I do, then don't you think I'm a genius?"

If you ask any parent in any country what they want most, academically, for their child, the answer will often be, "I want my child to love to read."

"My dads have read to me every night since I was born," Alex, the seven-year-old chef, told me one day. He loved books and, more than anything, loved to be read to. "I love hearing stories. I just wish I could read."

BECOMING A READER

During our years together, reading became one of our daily activities. At first, I read to Alex. As he became a reader, we read aloud to each other. I began with two of my favorites, *My Father's Dragon* and *Chocolate Fever*, and, as the years went by, Katherine Applegate's book, *The Home of the Brave*, about the Lost Boys of Sudan. This became Alex's favorite.

One night after I'd been working with Alex for three years, I got a call at 10 p.m. from Alex's dad. I'd never gotten a call like this from him. "Call me back as soon as you get this," Mitchell pleaded.

My family and I had just finished having a Seder for the Jewish holiday of Passover, and I wondered if the holiday had anything to do with the phone call. My Jewish students were always nervous—one of the activities at the Seder table is for each person to read from the book about the story of Passover. My students always described how uncomfortable and unhappy they were because they couldn't read at the table, their parents had to keep correcting them, and they were embarrassed to make mistakes in front of the company.

I called Mitchell. "What's up?" I asked.

He let out a short sob. "Alex read at the Seder table for the first time ever tonight! He read so well. We are totally amazed!"

I could only imagine how Alex felt. When I saw Alex later that week, he told me how proud he was that he really could *read*. For a child with learning differences who loves books, being unable to read is extremely upsetting. They may be thirsty for knowledge and are frustrated when people say, "You're so smart!" Because they can't read, they think, "How smart can I be if I can't read?"

Many programs teach reading, but you want your kids to *love* reading. Parents of nonreaders, who choose one of those intensive six-week reading programs popping up all over the country, find that their child may learn the basics of reading, but they never learn to love reading because instilling the love of reading isn't the goal. "He can sort of read," the parents always tell me later. "But he had a tantrum every time I took him there." That horrible program will probably give the child the gift of hating to read for the rest of his life!

When your child is young, you can instill a love of reading and a curiosity about learning by doing these simple things:

- Put them in your lap and open a bright-colored book and let the words flow.

- Read a sentence and stop at the last word. Your child will say the word because they had heard it so many times.

- Continue to read to your child as your child gets older. Rhyming books, color books, number books, animal books, and alphabet books help develop language skills early on.

> • "Read" wordless picture books, which are books with only pictures, no words. You show your child (even by three, if they can talk) the book and go through looking at the pictures. Then go through the book again and ask your child to tell you what's going on in the picture on each page.

As they grow up, you can type and print out what they dictate to you and paste the words on the pages of the book, or photocopy the book and paste the words. Your child has then become a writer, a real author! How proud they will be!

When my daughter, Ali, was 15 months old, I'd walk into her room in the morning and she'd be sitting in her crib holding a book and reading! She wasn't saying actual words, but babbling and turning the pages. She was pretend-reading all the books I had read to her.

> • Any time of day, find an excuse to read to your child.
>
> • Read books with opposites, idioms, compound words, and rhyming, and sing songs.
>
> • Read adventures, mysteries, fantasies, series books, humor, poetry, graphic novels, and non-fiction. Make sure the books you keep around are on topics that interest your child. They can be anything from glossy animal magazines to joke books.

- Write a message or a joke and put it in their lunchbox every day.

- You can also play audible books in the car. On YouTube they have sing-alongs with the words on the screen.

- Cook with your child and read the recipes.

- Go to places that have storytelling hours. Still stumped? Your librarian is a fantastic reference.

- Take books when you leave the house. Bring them to restaurants and give books to your child when you're in the car.

Share reading with your child even through to adulthood. My son would drag books to his crib and put them at the end of the bed. In the morning I'd wake up and he'd be sitting up in his crib "reading." I'm still sending interesting articles to my 40-year-old adult children. If you haven't been reading to your child, there's no time like the present to begin!

Reading to your child expands their vocabulary. You can talk about what words mean, always in the context of a sentence, after you've read to them. Even if your child is four years old, if the animal you just read about hibernates, tell them what that means. If you introduce questioning as part of reading, children can be taught to think critically.

When reading a story, you might ask:

- Who are the characters?

- What is the setting?

- Where does the book begin?

- What happens at the end?

- What problem are the characters facing?

I call this type of questioning "reading the lines" of a story—just telling the facts.

You can also check their comprehension by waiting a bit to ask about the facts. For instance, if you read a story together before bed, next morning on the way to school, you can ask your child to retell the story. You might have read a story about a boy who has no friends and no one to talk to. He wants a dog, but his parents won't give him one because they are afraid he won't walk, feed, and train it. The boy does all this with his stuffed dog, so his parents agree to give him a real dog. At the end of the story, he goes to bed, and the dog says, "Good night, friend."

Some beginning questions:

- Who is the main character in the story?

- What did the boy want?

- How did the boy finally get the dog?

You might ask your child to draw three pictures of the story in sequence. Use the actual word "sequence" and then ask, "What happened first, next, and last?"

You can then move on to critical thinking questions, which are interpretative questions that I call "reading between the lines." I am far more interested in my students being able to read between the lines.

Questions in this category include:

- Have you ever wanted something so badly?

- Could a boy want a dog and get it?

- Could a dog talk?

- How does the story make you feel?

- Have you ever read a book like this?

- *What would be another title for this story?*

You're asking them to interpret, compare, and contrast. You don't have to ask all these questions about one book, but these are the types of critical thinking questions you can ask.

The third type of questioning is "reading beyond the lines." These questions are even more sophisticated in terms of critical thinking skills and there are no "right" answers. It may shock you that your child is capable of answering these, even at a young age, but children with learning differences are often very deep thinkers. They are always the ones in class who can answer the most difficult comprehension questions. This has been true for all my students, whether I was teaching in the inner city of Detroit, in Virginia, Ohio, or California.

Beyond-the-line questions go beyond the story. They connect the literature to the child's own experiences. "What would you do in the same situation?" No child is too young to answer this question. In fact, I have asked these questions of three-year-olds. And they can answer them.

My favorite question among them is: "What's going to happen next?" It shows me if the child understands what has happened so far and can interpret the story and predict the future. "Will the dog wake up the next morning and talk? Was the boy imagining it?" You can share your opinions, too. In our story about the boy and dog, I think the boy is imagining that the dog talks, but my student might want the dog to continue talking in the morning. You can also have them continue the story by writing, drawing, or dictating to you what they think will happen. Appendix A has a list of comprehension questions. Find the ones you are comfortable asking.

> Some suggestions for you:
>
> - Most children I teach with learning differences do not visualize as they read. But children who make pictures in their minds as they read get more out of a book. After a page is read, I ask them to "see" the story, describe the boy, his dog, his house. If a child does it enough, eventually they learn to do it automatically. That is one of the most important skills I teach them. The visualizing helps them "see" the story and remember it.

- You can also compare books. There are many books about dogs with issues. Kids love them. *Bark, George,* by Jules Feiffer, is about a dog who, when asked to bark, doesn't bark but makes another animal sound. *Walter the Farting Dog,* by William Kotzwinkle and Glenn Murray, is about a dog with a terrible case of flatulence. Read one book one night and the other the next, then talk about the two dogs. How are they alike or different? Children love books with animals or characters who have challenges. It makes them realize even animals and other people have challenges, too!

- Become familiar with the most wonderful place in the world, the library. I always find that children's librarians will talk to your child and help them choose books. They also know the books that are most popular. Make visiting the library a habit. Most libraries have sales on books that people have donated, and I have found my favorite books for 50 cents to a dollar.

- Using your child's favorite book, you might suggest doing an art project about it or writing a song about it. You can take an empty cardboard box and have them make something from the story they have read. Doing a short project in the aftermath lets you know they understood it. For the dog story, my student took a large Amazon box and made it into a flying car so the boy and dog could fly anywhere they wanted.

- If your child loves technology, they can make a film on their iPhone about the book or make clay characters from the book. Whatever your child likes to do, incorporate reading. Keep a notebook on the books they've read and have them rate them with one to five stars, as they do on Goodreads.

- As your child gets older, try to read the books they are required to read for school. It makes for some interesting family discussions. Share your feelings about the books. You can always find summaries of the book online if you need to review it.

Whatever you do, don't make reading with your child feel like work. It should be enjoyable. You want your child to *love* reading, not hate it. And by that process, you can remain their loving parent, rather than their teacher. You are there to love your child whether they can read or not, and when reading to your child, ask questions, play word and alphabet games, and do projects around books. Do it because you love them, and you are hoping they will love reading, not because you are trying to teach them.

In my experience, as soon as a parent tries to "teach" their child, the child feels compromised, and crying meltdowns and oppositional behavior can result. You may wind up having a child who is against anything associated with reading and writing.

Teachers will use different skills that you won't have to. For instance, a teacher will probably use "decoding," which means teaching students to sound out a word, if they don't know it, by taking the word apart sound by sound. I caution parents *not* to try to teach decoding because many students have speech issues and cannot pronounce sounds correctly, so trying to sound out words is difficult. And blending sounds can be impossible with a speech issue. This part of teaching reading is best left up to therapists and teachers. Phonemic awareness—hearing individual sounds in words—is also best left to professionals.

Most important, if you are noticing that your child is having trouble reading, just make sure their hearing (can they hear the words?), vision (do they need glasses?), and speech (do they have any trouble making certain sounds?) are checked. All these can contribute to a tough time learning to read.

My students love being read to. They love great stories with great characters. They like characters with problems they can relate to. And they love predicting outcomes. They usually can retell the entire story, including the elements of the story: the characters, what the problem was, and the conclusion. They especially like nonfiction. All the large *National Geographic* books or the *Weird but True!* series are favorites. They like it when I read the news to them from *Newsela* or *The Week Junior* so we can discuss what's happening in the world. And they like humor—whether it's a book of jokes or a book filled with funny idioms. My students eventually learn to *love* to read.

The most interesting fact I teach students and their parents is that half of every page in every printed material is composed of the 100 most common words. These are called high-frequency words. Edward Fry, an educator who taught at Rutgers University, researched and found which words ranked in order of frequency. The first 100 words make up approximately half of all the words found in newspapers, textbooks, children's stories, and novels. Just 25 words make up a third of all written material published, and the first 300 words make up 65% of all written material. In fact, only 13 words account for 25% of all words in print. After my students successfully learn the first 100 words, I can take any book in my room and have them read a page; this boosts their confidence as they realize that they can now read at least half of any given page put before them, all because of learning the high-frequency words. You can find this list of 100 high-frequency words in appendix B. Talk about giving children power and confidence!

High-frequency words can be memorized so they are automatically recognized by your child. They should be recognized as a whole and not require any word analysis for reading them.

A Reading Sleepover

As the reading teacher at a school in Los Angeles, I planned a yearly event with my 50 reading center students. We executed a reading sleepover in the big gymnasium at my school. Children came to school at five in the evening with their favorite reading material (a book or magazines) and their sleeping bag and pajamas. They read for half an hour, then for the next half hour did a reading-related activity that was fun. We had dinner and met a book author I had invited to the sleepover.

One year, Stephen Cosgrove, author of 325 *Serendipity* books, came and entertained the students in the evening before bed.

Eve Bunting, a children's book author of over 250 books, heard about the event, came to interview me, and wrote a best-selling book called *Sixth-Grade Sleepover*. The event in the book was just like mine and the teacher's characteristics were copied after me!

You can plan a reading sleepover at home with some friends. The children bring books and sleeping bags, have dinner, read, and do fun reading activities during the night. It's always a big hit and another way to help your child feel good about reading.

THE TAKEAWAY

There isn't one method that will magically teach your child to read. For a child with reading difficulties, learning to read must be taught by a professional trained in working with children with learning differences. These professionals have an eclectic approach to teaching that helps with decoding, comprehension, fluency, listening, vocabulary, and writing.

But there's still plenty of room for *you*, as a parent, to instill a love of reading and learning in your child, regardless of what their learning differences may be. Use the ideas in this chapter to foster a love of reading and make it fun!

[9]

Does It Matter
What Your Child Reads?

From Comic Books to Pokémon Cards

Actor Tom Cruise was not only bullied in school for his differences but was often frustrated and bored. This is all too common with smart kids whose differences aren't being recognized and accounted for.

———————— // ————————

I never worried about what my own children or my students were reading as long as they were *reading*! I read to my firstborn, Andrew, every single day in utero, the second he came out, and all through his young life. I read him magazines, poetry, jokes, fiction, and nonfiction books. At 15 months, when he was hardly talking, I would read him stories and leave out the last word of a sentence so that he would say the word that fit into the sentence. He did this because he was read to every day, so he knew the way language worked.

As Andrew got older, reading chapter books was a nighttime ritual. I'd won a contest and received 200 books from a publisher, and I read most of them to Andrew. In February during his second-grade year (39 years ago), he began to read on his own. He became a voracious reader of . . . comic books. He collected them, read and reread them. He was never without a comic book in his hands. Comic books blend words and pictures, a great combination. I was still reading books to him, but he never picked up a book.

Reading comes in many forms.

My husband kept watching him like the dad tiger in Robert Kraus's *Leo the Late Bloomer* for Andrew's signs of "blooming." Just like the tiger mom in the story, I kept saying, "He'll bloom in his own time. Andrew is reading—even if it's comic books or 1,000 baseball cards or Pokémon cards, he's still reading. When the passion for reading comic books passes, he'll be used to reading, so he will turn to other forms of reading."

IT ALL WORKED OUT

This turned out to be true. Andrew now reads all the time and shares that love with my grandson, Nick. Nick was also read to every night, but he would not pick up a book on his own. Then one day Nick became a voracious "reader" of . . . audible books! The iPad is not allowed with grandma so I bought him audible books to listen to on the long ride home from his school to our home.

In June of Nick's second-grade year, his mom said, "But he's not reading."

"It is a different form of reading," I told her. "But audible books are still books, and he loves stories so much, he'll start picking up actual books to read soon."

In July, while Nick was on summer vacation, I received a picture of him with a stack of books he'd just read. His note read, "Hi Grandma! I read 20 books this summer!"

POKÉMON: YES! THAT'S READING!

Audible books, comic books, graphic novels, and the craze of collecting Pokémon cards can all motivate your child to want to read. The oldies are still on all the best children's book lists. When a book is good, it's good no matter how old it is. Check websites like Common Sense Media and Scholastic Books or Reading Rockets for updates on book lists. If it says a book is good for nine-year-olds, that may mean your child might be able to read it, but I have found that children five and six might like hearing the book read to them because they can't read yet. Also, be sure to check the interest level and subject matter to make sure it is appropriate for your child.

Most of the children I see from age four until seven collect Pokémon cards. The Pokémon Company was created by Satoshi in Japan over 23 years ago as a game in which Pokémon trainers catch fictional creatures ("pocket monsters") and train them to battle each other for sport. Each character has a made-up name. And each name can be decoded (sounded out) as children can do when they come to an unfamiliar word.

Children are taught about long-vowel sounds in school. Show your child Bayleef and Beedrill Pokémon and tell them they have the long-vowel sound of *e* like in "street" and "meet." Your child will listen, and I can guarantee you they'll remember the sound because it relates to their Pokémon characters.

Another skill Pokémon teaches is the blends in words; that is, two or three consonants that say their sound when you read them (spr, bl, fl, fr, gr, etc.). The Pokémon characters *Blastoise*, *Floatzel*, *Frillish*, and *Granbull* all begin with blends.

"I CAN DO THAT!"

Pokémon started as video games and trading cards and now has evolved into trading card games, TV shows, movies, books, an incredibly popular app, and numerous toys. A 2016 Pokémon commercial had the theme "I can do that!"

Of course, as an educator, I've seen how important it is when my students say "I can do that" instead of "I can't do that."

The Pokémon Essential Handbook has every character listed in alphabetical order, and on each page there is a "how to say it" phrase that tells the reader how to pronounce the character's name.

Here are some ideas of what to do with those hundreds of Pokémon cards:

- Make a chart on poster board, listing every Pokémon character your child likes. Have them write a real word under the Pokémon name that has the same sound as the character. For example: Pikachu has the *ch* digraph. Under his name your child might write "chocolate" or "chip," which have the *ch* sound. I have never had a child not want to list real words under the character. What a great way to combine a love of Pokémon and real words!

- Have your child make up stories with the Pokémon characters. Type their story, print it out, and put all the stories in a three-ring binder. They'll love going back and "reading" their stories. Your child, who loves Pokémon, will want to be able to pronounce all the sounds!

- Have your child put all the Pokémon cards in alphabetical order, or make a bingo game with character names in all 25 spaces. Then add real words with the same sounds under each character name. You are using what they love without really teaching. Children think "fun" rather than "work."

With each new child I meet who has a special passion, I discover new books I love. It happened just this week when I met a five-year-old, Sandi. When I asked her mom the first time I talked to her what Sandi loved, her mom replied, "Fairy tales and princesses." I took out all my fairy tale books, which included the actual fairy tales and then modern-day versions of fairy tales, such as *Computerella*, which, as strange as it seems, is from 1992 and about a prince who searches throughout the kingdom to find the perfect person to fix the royal computer. Another favorite modern-day fairy tale was written by William Wegman, who used his own dogs dressed up as the characters.

I hadn't met Sandi so I wasn't sure which books she'd like. But I was ready with several. I was surprised that Sandi, with no pets at home, picked Wegman's *Cinderella* with all his real-life dogs dressed as characters. Her mom texted me later that night: "Sandi had me read the Wegman book three times, then begged to take it to sleep with her. Don't worry. I took the dust jacket off before tucking her in with the book!"

FINDING THE RIGHT BOOK(S)

What makes one child love one book or have one passion or another, I will never know. But most children are very particular in their likes and dislikes of stories.

If you are lucky enough to have a children's book store near you, take your child there for a few hours. Ask the owner or salesperson what books they suggest based on your child's passions and age. I can assure you even a four-year-old will know exactly what books they want to hear.

Reading includes anything from listening to a story being read to listening to a book on an audible app to reading graphic novels, joke books, *Weird but True!* books, the LEGO magazines, *National Geographic Kids* magazine, *Ranger Rick, The Week Junior,* comics, and Pokémon cards. It's all *reading,* and if your child likes stories, they will eventually begin to read books, too.

THE TAKEAWAY

Not long ago, I bumped into one of my previous students, Isabella. I still work with her brothers, but I wondered how she was doing. "Do you still like graphic novels?" I asked her. "I love them," she replied. "But Dad will only allow me to read 'real books,' not graphic novels." I looked at her dad and replied, "You let your boys play Minecraft and kill people with guns, but you won't allow your daughter to read graphic novels? Something is wrong with this picture."

My girl students love the graphic novels of *The Baby-Sitters Club* series. The original series by Ann M. Martin has 131 titles with 176 million books in print. After finishing all the graphic novels, they then read all the actual babysitter books! Graphic novels are reading. Once a child is reading, whether it's comic books or *Dog Man* or the babysitter graphic novels, they've become a reader and will continue reading!

[10]

For the Love of Writing

Richard Branson is an English business magnate and investor who founded Virgin Group and in 2021 flew to the edge of space in a spacecraft. He has learning differences and has said, "My teachers labeled me as lazy or not very clever." He started a newspaper in school and the headmaster told him, "I predict you'll go to prison or become a millionaire." Branson has said, "It isn't a disability, just a different way of thinking."

———————————— // ————————————

In all the years that I have taught students with learning differences, reading comes sooner than writing. Writing involves many skills that unfortunately my students often lack. "I hate to write," Alex told me when he was seven years old. He could cook a fabulous pizza and create artistic masterpieces out of old cameras and junk from my garage, but he couldn't hold his pencil or form letters correctly, and he wasn't able to spell.

But Alex was interested in all things newsworthy so as he grew, I'd read him unusual pieces from *The Week* magazine whenever he came to see me. What child wouldn't be interested in short articles about a dentist who performs root canals on lions, a glass church shaped like a shoe, or a golden retriever who could drive a moped? And best of all, a whole article about Pokémon turning 20!

WHY NOT WRITE A LETTER?

When Alex turned nine and went to sleepaway camp, I kept sending him funny articles from *The Week* magazine. When he got back from camp, I asked if he'd read all the letters he got. "Only yours because of *The Week* articles." I suggested he write William Falk, the editor of *The Week*, to tell him. Alex typed the letter, and Mr. Falk emailed him in less than an hour, saying how much he'd enjoyed his letter!

Now the Falk story is a great one, but the road to writing that letter took a long time. As mentioned, writing involves a combination of certain skills that students with learning differences lack. Often a teacher suggests a writing idea students may not be interested in and about which they then have to think of something to write. Then they have to get the words on paper. Many students have physical challenges actually writing, and so they can't write the letters correctly or get the words on the lines. If they have speech differences and can't pronounce a word correctly, they tend to spell the word wrong.

After all this, when they finally do get a sentence down, they often don't remember what else they wanted to write and give up. What has been produced is a sentence the teacher can't read because the letters are all over the page and the words are spelled incorrectly. The child can't read it back, even though he thought of the words, because he doesn't see letters or words that are correctly written. Thinking of an idea to write, remembering what you want to write, staying focused on the idea, physically forming the letters, and hearing the sounds and spelling the words is a lot to ask for.

My five-year-old student Sarah came into my house and announced, "I'm not going to be Rapunzel when I grow up . . . I'm going to be a writer!"

START EARLY

Early intervention, as I've stated throughout the book, is the key. And your child will find an easier time typing (keyboarding) on the computer than writing by hand. By the end of second grade most schools are teaching typing. There are online typing sites that are fun for your child. They can practice 10 minutes a night and eventually become proficient. Typing increases processing speed so that your child can actually type their thoughts down. The only glitch is that if your child has speech issues, then spell check will be more difficult for them unless they know the sounds of the words.

So, how do I get my students to write? I always teach to their passions and strengths. When meeting a student for the first time, I talk about something they're interested in. Alex loved pandas, so I logged on to the Smithsonian website and we watched the new baby on the Panda Cam. Then I read Alex an article about pandas from the *National Geographic* magazine for kids. Afterward, I took out a piece of lined second-grade paper. I saw the shock on his face. "But I can't write or spell."

"What did you like best about what you just saw on the Panda Cam and in the article we read?"

He immediately told me five facts, and I wrote them on the paper. Then I pointed to each word and he *read* what he had dictated to me.

"I can read?" He looked a bit shocked. I confirmed he did actually read.

Children with learning differences can dictate stories and thoughts to a parent or teacher, especially if it is a topic they are interested in. Usually they can "read" it back because the topic is interesting to them and they remember what they said.

I found a fascinating article about an animal called the civet and brought it into my office to read to Alex, who was still a nonreader and, as I've said, very smart. I read him the article, and when I finished, we both said, "Ugggg, gross." It was such a funny reaction from both of us. Then I asked Alex to tell me the most interesting parts of the article, and I typed them for him. He dictated: "A civet is an animal who eats ripe coffee cherries. Then it poops it out and the poop is made into coffee that costs $200 a cup."

"Would you ever drink that?" Alex asked.

"No way," I replied.

"Let's go to Google and see if we can get it in Los Angeles," he said. "Look. You can get it at a coffee shop for $50."

"Well, that's cheaper than $200," I said.

"Let's go there on a field trip," Alex laughed.

"Are you allowed to drink coffee, especially made from poop?" I asked.

"No," he answered. "But I'd like to see you do it."

I squished my face and yelled, "Ugggh!" and "Oohhhh!" and "No way!"

ASK FOR HELP FROM YOUR TEAM

Read your child articles or books they may like. The more you read to them, the more knowledge your child will learn, the more they will have to write about in school, and the more comfortable they will feel when the teacher asks them to do a writing assignment. Eventually adding in typing will make their life easier.

I find my students will do anything with me, but if I give them homework to do with a parent, I get a call saying the child is crying and doesn't want to work. Students don't always want their parents to help with their writing assignments. Ask your child's teacher or involve your child's educational specialist to help with written assignments. It is of utmost importance that your child loves their therapist. If they love their educational specialist, they will work hard for them.

Most teachers have a certain way they want a report done. Find out how they want it done and how they grade. There should be communication between the teacher, the educational specialist, and the parent for a child with issues to succeed in writing.

Below are a few pointers about writing assignments:

- Talk to your child when a writing assignment is given. Let them verbally tell you what they want to write about.

- If it is a topic the teacher assigned that they don't know much about, help them find books about it or go to the internet and find interesting articles about the topic.

- After reading the articles, ask your child to tell you what they thought was most interesting.

- Get color-coded index cards and start having your child write the most interesting facts on the cards. You can talk about a topic sentence, the facts, and the ending to their report.

- If your child gets upset, you can do the research together and let the educational specialist help with the actual writing.

- Do not be critical or negative. At this point, you just want your child to see they are able to find interesting facts, and you can try to help them begin to organize.

- The editing process is when I introduce juicy adjectives and capitalization, punctuation and paragraph structure, and help them expand their vocabulary by using a kids' thesaurus.

My students love the part of a report when they get to create a visual to go with their writing because most of my students like the freedom to create. Even so, you may have to ask your child what they want to make and help them organize things, get the materials, and decide how to put it together. Many of my students have executive functioning differences, too, so doing this with them helps them learn how to do a report with a project. (See chapter 11 on executive functioning.)

Apart from homework, the way to build a child's confidence in writing is to try to make the writing process as enjoyable as you can. My suggestion is to write with your child outside school and make it *fun*:

- Buy a bulletin board that goes in their room, family room, or playroom. Even if your child is only two years old, their "writing" (dictating to you) can be put up on the bulletin board. You want your child to be confident. The "I can do it" is what you want to hear. If it's fun, believe me, they will learn.

- Start when your child has some language so they can tell you what they want you to write. After you go on an outing to the park, play with a friend, or go swimming, ask your child to finish these sentences: Today I _____. I played with _____. We went to the _____. Print it in big letters on a piece of construction paper and print out your favorite picture of the day at the park and put it on the paper.

- Take pictures of your child's birthday party. Buy a hardcover book with empty pages from Ashley on Amazon. Have your child paste the pictures of the party in sequence in the book. Ask them: "What did we do first? What did we do second? Then what?" Write what they say under the picture. Your child will see there is a sequence in stories. You can tell a story with pictures and a sentence—all you want to do is involve your child in the act of writing.

- After reading a story to your child, have them tell you the name of the story, who the characters were, where the story took place, if there was a problem, what it was, and what happened at the end. Children who love being read to can answer these questions. The elements of a story, or the 5 Ws and H (who, what, when, where, why, how), are taught in every elementary classroom. You can divide a paper into five or six squares and have your child draw pictures of the story. Write the words your child dictates about the story.

- From a young age, ask your child to make a birthday card for relatives. Do not correct the spelling. You want your child to enjoy writing, not think of it as a teaching lesson.

- On a message board in your kitchen, write a sentence a day. Your child will look forward to knowing what it says.

- Find old cameras, parts of old cameras, parts of computers, or TV remotes at flea markets, or ask at camera shops for broken cameras. Have your child create a character and tell you which parts they want hot glued. (Glue guns are *very* hot. Only an adult can use one, and even then, be careful!) You can use empty toilet paper rolls or any fun art supplies to add to the camera parts. It can be an imaginary character or one they love already from their favorite book. Then they can write a story, or dictate one to you, about their character.

- In school they are learning different kinds of writing, and you can help them practice these.

  - *Persuasive:* Ask your child to write why you should buy them something. My favorite is having kids write or dictate why they should have a cell phone!

  - *Fact and opinion:* Tell me a fact. And what did you like or dislike about the story or book?

  - *Informative:* What fact about which animal did you like in *The Week Junior* magazine I just read to you?

Online there are thousands of topic sentences for writing at different ages. Don't correct or criticize your child's writing. All you want to do is make the writing something they like to do.

Keep teaching to their passions!

The very best thing you can do is to continually read to your child at home. This opens the windows to writing.

It was the third year into my working with Alex. He was now in fourth grade. He was reading, but writing still was difficult for all the reasons mentioned above. We read Katherine Applegate's book *The Home of the Brave*, about a boy from Sudan who comes to the United States. She is a powerful writer who also wrote *The One and Only Ivan*, about the gorilla who lived in a shopping mall. She fictionalizes real events. Alex loved the book about the lost boy, and when we finished we went to YouTube to watch a *60 Minutes* story about the Lost Boys of Sudan. The next day his dad, Mitchell, emailed me. He told me he drove his four children to school, and it was Alex's turn to sit in the front. Alex said, "I have to read you this poem from my book. It's so good." Alex opened the book and read "Snow," a poem by the lost boy from Sudan about the first time he saw snow.

Mitchell said he almost cried to hear his son reading, and he was even more delighted to have him start up a conversation with his siblings about the Lost Boys and immigration.

THE TAKEAWAY

Not long after this, Alex's teacher was talking about similes. When we were reading *The Home of the Brave*, I had showed Alex how it was filled with similes, so he was familiar with them. The teacher asked the children to write something using similes. In a few minutes Alex wrote:

"The Lost Boy of Sudan, thin like a chopstick, arrived in Minnesota. The air, cold like ice, pinched his cheeks. The social worker greeted Kek with a handshake and gave him gloves. Kek didn't know what to do with the furry hands the man gave him. They looked like they were severed hands from a monkey.

Kek moved into a small apartment with his aunt and cousin, but he thought it was as big as a castle. He became friends with Hannah, a girl as lonely as an apple fallen from a tree to the empty ground below."

These words were not written by a student who didn't understand what was going on in class or the book he read. He saw how the author used similes all throughout the book, which helped inspire him as he wrote those paragraphs.

There was no doubt about it, Alex had become a writer. And your child will, too, if you use what they're interested in to write about, and you find stories about subjects they're interested in.

[11]

Understanding
Executive Functioning

Daymond John, *Shark Tank* investor, businessman, and
CEO of fashion label FUBU, says that he didn't let his
learning differences define him. He used his strengths to
get ahead. Parlaying love of what you do into success is at
the heart of what I teach.

———————————— // ————————————

It is obvious that Daymond, who made his fortune making
hats and clothes, was able to overcome his learning differences and take the steps needed to make his clothing line
a success: set goals, start tasks, stay focused, and follow

directions. He was able to use his executive functioning to succeed and fulfill his dreams.

Executive functioning is sometimes called "the management system of the brain." The term refers to a collection of related skills, notably memory, organization, and focusing on tasks and goals. Self-awareness and self-regulation are key to mastering this "system." My student Chris is a good example of a very smart child who had trouble with executive functioning. Chris had been adopted at 14 months. His parents told me right from the beginning that Chris was a hard baby to soothe. He didn't sleep well, was always running around, couldn't focus on a toy or story for very long, was impulsive, and was hard to understand when he spoke.

In kindergarten Chris had difficulty recognizing and writing his letters and often used his body and hands to interact with classmates. Because he wasn't focused, he didn't hear the teacher's directions (auditory memory), had poor visual memory (remembering the sounds of letters to decode a new word), and also had severe speech issues, so he couldn't hear sounds in a word to be able to decode it.

Because Chris was not getting the help and attention he needed in a traditional classroom, his parents agreed to have him tested by a neuropsychologist, and he was diagnosed with learning differences and ADHD. Medication was suggested, and the parents agreed to have Chris try them. The parents also upped our sessions to three hours a week. Chris never complained.

The medicine made a huge difference. Chris was able to focus, and that helped him learn to read. He loved reading. Though he still had difficulties getting his millions of ideas from his brain to paper because his hand couldn't form letters correctly, he was able to tell me what he had learned and loved in something he read, and I typed what he dictated to me. The meds helped his impulsivity and attention. He wasn't hitting others in times of stress. He started to make friends, and he was very attentive in our sessions. He frequently would walk into each session and say, "What's in the news this week?"

ADAPT AS YOUR CHILD GETS OLDER

But when Chris entered the third grade, his work got a lot harder. Executive functioning becomes very difficult for some students in the third grade. Students have to read very differently in third grade than in first and second grades, and there are a lot of books to read, facts to remember, and reports to be written. The meds helped him pay attention, but he still had to organize information from all his classes in a binder, remember what to do each night, plan time to do his homework, plan extra time for writing—which was still difficult—and figure out what was important and when to study for tests. It was tough to retain in his memory all the information that he read and that his teacher gave him and then transfer it to the work he was doing. Through all this, he tried not to have a tantrum, get upset, or give up.

In grades three through six, students like Chris, who have executive functioning issues, often hit a wall if they are not helped. Your child, even if they've learned to read and write, might need an educational specialist for the upper grades if they want to continue learning the difficult skills of executive functioning.

Luckily, Chris wound up excelling in third grade because his teacher had incredible ways of teaching executive functioning. She had the children follow her outlines and answer her exact questions. Chris was able to begin improving in executive functioning because he had his teacher's help, the help of his team, and the right medication.

After third grade, Chris went to summer camp. I'd written him about the soccer boys stuck in the cave in Thailand. When he got back, he wanted to know all about the soccer boys. He was also interested in how the goliath grouper, a 500-pound fish, ate a shark during his time away at camp. Before school, he wrote a report on the soccer boys and the grouper. After all this hard work, he now enjoyed excellent executive functioning skills.

"Executive functioning" is a very significant term when discussing students with learning differences. The signs of executive functioning disorder can look like ADHD because ADHD is actually a problem with executive functioning. When a child has executive functioning disorder, it's difficult for them to:

- Set goals.
- Start tasks.
- Stay focused.
- Remember and follow directions.
- Organize, plan, and prioritize.
- Stay level-headed during stress.

Because being able to stay focused on a task is so important to executive functioning, one of the best things you can do is to figure out what your child loves. Working with a child on what they love or are interested in makes it easier for them to stay on task, remember what they want to do, organize their thoughts, and stay level during times when they are challenged.

A ROLLER-COASTER RIDE TO SUCCESS

When Eddie, another one of my students who struggled with executive functioning, was in third grade, the doctor concluded that Eddie should be on medication. Eddie had learned to read and write, but he was difficult to teach. He was impulsive and often said, "I don't want to do this." Eddie's dad refused to put him on any medication because he'd been just like Eddie as a child and said he'd turned out fine. When I asked Eddie about his passions, he was the only student who ever said, "Roller coasters."

Eddie's grandmother lived near Cedar Point, Ohio, where some of the biggest roller coasters in the world are. Eddie knew the name of each one, their heights, how long the first drop was, their length, and inversions. That year, his third-grade teacher gave each child a subject to work on. Eddie was given strawberries. It was really tough trying to get Eddie to think about strawberries. He didn't care about strawberries, and it felt like a punishment, trying to sit down and learn about them. Finally, I wrote to the teacher and asked if Eddie could possibly do his project on roller coasters instead. She replied, "Yes."

Eddie was totally motivated about doing a report on something he loved. I looked at roller coasters and got dizzy, but Eddie googled roller coasters and visited the Cedar Point website. He immediately began writing and making a chart of all the rides, characteristics, and how tall you had to be to ride them. You had to be 52 inches to ride the big coasters and Eddie was 48 inches. He was getting ready to go visit his grandmother, and his mom promised to take him to Cedar Point.

Eddie's executive functioning skills continued to develop on his trip to Cedar Point to visit his grandma. He took his notebook with him with questions he'd devised to ask people he met, coaster operators and anyone else from the park. The question he was most excited about was how people rate the coasters—a big deal to coaster enthusiasts.

He came back with a decision to not only write his report but design a roller coaster and construct one to go with his report. This idea took a tremendous amount of executive functioning skill. He made a huge book (3 feet by 3 feet) with pictures of coasters he'd imagined, using real math dimensions. Then with boxes and junk from my garage, he built a model mini roller coaster.

In an amazing coincidence, the next weekend there was an article in the *New York Times* about Rob Decker, one of the biggest roller-coaster designers in the world, whose office was at Cedar Point. The discoverer of the *Titanic*, Robert Ballard, had written to my *Titanic*-obsessed student after I'd found him, and I thought Eddie might have a chance at a correspondence with Rob Decker.

Eddie loved the idea of writing to Rob and had many questions to ask, including "What is your favorite roller coaster?" and "I design roller coasters, too. Can I work for you when I'm 52 inches tall?" and "My mom and I went on a roller coaster, and my mom's sunglasses flew off, and I lost my hat. How can we get them back?"

Rob answered with a lovely letter to Eddie and a virtual video of a new roller coaster being built for the park. Rob's answer to the sunglasses and hat question was that he had no idea, so he'd called the park and was told all Eddie's mom had to do was call Cedar Point Lost and Found and they'd send the items back. Unclaimed items were donated to people in need, so even if they weren't still there, they were at least with people who needed them!

Watching the virtual reality video of the new coaster planned for the park made me really dizzy. Eddie said I could go with them to Cedar Point next time he went. I replied, "Never." Eddie, waiting to be 52 inches, will be the first one on board, with his brave mom (hopefully not wearing designer sunglasses!).

HOW TO DEVELOP EXECUTIVE FUNCTIONING

There are many ways to teach executive functioning to children using their passions. Eddie's third-grade teacher could have passed out questionnaires to the students at the beginning of the year, asking what passions they had instead of assigning arbitrary topics like strawberries. Most elementary school students are passionate about something, and I doubt it is strawberries.

Many students love cooking, animals, space, Disney, Google, football, soccer, basketball, filmmaking, LEGO sets, Matchbox cars, music, creating stories, acting, singing, poetry, the *Titanic*, entering contests, baseball, science, and anything to do with creating things with their hands. If the object is to teach a child to use his or her executive functioning skills, let the child choose a topic.

Any subject where a child has to do a project around building something involves executive functioning and can be accomplished with LEGO bricks. They can be used for any project at school, too.

Nathan, whom I taught for four years, from first to fifth grade, worked with a team, including me, and was on medication. But when he entered fifth grade his parents decided he could work on his own, using no therapists. Though he'd turned into a great reader and writer, he still had many difficulties with executive functioning in middle school. He had to be able to research a topic, decide on what information he wanted to use, and write the report. It was also hard for him to figure out how to do all the work in his five separate classes. His parents finally hired an educational specialist to help him with his executive functioning, and it helped tremendously.

Even if medication aids your child in accessing their executive functions better, issues will still be there, especially as the workload from school increases. Continue using your resources, even if your child seems to be in a good rhythm in school.

Ways to Work on Executive Functioning at Home:

- Show your child how to use their planner from school or use technology sites with calendars to make a list of what they have to do. Plan out their class work each week.

- If they have to do a report, help them find articles and books and read the resources with them. Use index cards or the computer to record the important points.

- Find out when tests are being given and begin studying days before instead of the night before. Nathan had a states test and began preparing just two nights before. There was no way he could learn all the states and put them on a blank map in two days. It brought on panic and a difficulty in self-control, which can come with executive functioning challenges.

- Plan a trip with the family. This includes many executive functioning skills: where to go, what to pack, and what activities to do on the trip.

- Even playing video games like Minecraft and Fortnight, a child has to use executive functioning skills. Of course, I'm not so sure *just* doing video games transfers executive functioning skills to schoolwork! But it is one tool.

- Keep boxes. I love Amazon boxes! They are terrific for creative activities. I keep a stock in my garage. I have never had a child who didn't want to create something from a story they read, a story they heard, or a story they made up. I've seen life-size cars, *Star Wars* spaceships, and games with vocabulary on bean bags. (My student made a game throwing bean bags with words on them into a huge refrigerator box.) The most amazing sight is when I take a child into the myriad of "stuff" I have in the garage to create. Talk about executive functioning! They look for about 10 minutes and then whip together the most creative project. Deciding what to do, gathering all the materials they need, then putting it together and writing a story all require executive functioning skills.

Cooking is another activity that strengthens executive functioning. Alex, my cooking student, even at seven years old, was able to decide on the recipe he wanted to make, set out the ingredients, follow directions, and mix correctly (well, not always). When we were finished, I had Alex tell me what he liked about the recipe: Was it good? Did it need more of some ingredient, or was there something we could do next time to make it better?

If your child likes to cook, think of all the executive functioning skills that cooking entails, including reading the recipe, writing the grocery list, organizing the ingredients, setting them out, and following directions. If you happen to know a chef, ask if the chef would allow your child to come to the restaurant to see how it all works.

Nancy Silverton owns a restaurant here in Los Angeles. I have known her for 40 years. Alex the chef put on his chef's jacket and hat and we went to Nancy's restaurant. He followed her around for one night. On the way home I asked him what the best part was and he said, "How hard Nancy worked." And I answered, "If you work hard, you can succeed. Does that apply to you?" And Alex answered, "Yes. I have to keep working, but I also have to love what I do and Nancy really loves it." Wise words from a third grader.

THE TAKEAWAY

The more professionals learn about executive function differences and ADHD, the more closely they see them as linked. The frustrations so often experienced by children with undiagnosed ADHD can be similar to, or exacerbated by, specific executive function challenges with memory, planning, and seeing goals through to completion. Awareness of these challenges can help you and your team set your child up for success.

Remember this: sometimes educational specialists work better with students than parents do. Children get emotional and lack patience when being taught by a parent.

And keep in mind that communication with teachers is of utmost importance. They can tell you when tests will be given or when book reports and homework are due.

Children like Chris, Eddie, and Nathan, all of them extremely smart, with supportive parents and a team, are never totally through with therapies in executive functioning while they are in school. But when your child gets the accommodations they need, and develops the self-awareness to recognize and manage their executive function differences, they gain valuable confidence that will last a lifetime.

[12]

Four Types
of Processing

Kelly Ripa, actress and talk-show host, has a son with learning differences. She recalls how important finding the right school has been to her child's success: "I went to his new school for a parent-teacher conference and he's getting straight A's. I broke down crying in the middle of the conference."

———————————— // ————————————

On the report from the professional who evaluated your child, there might be one or more of these four types of processing issues. The first one, slow processing speed, is the most common, but the others may be included in the testing of your child, too. They include:

- Slow processing speed
- Sensory processing
- Auditory processing
- Visual processing

SLOW PROCESSING SPEED

Roger's parents kept getting reports back from his teacher that he never participated in class.

"Do you know the answers?" I asked Roger.

Roger was staring out the window at my huge silk oak tree as though daydreaming. Finally, he nodded. "But it takes me too long to answer," he explained, shrugging.

We practiced answering questions. I asked him questions about sharks and told him to raise his hand when he knew the answer. Of course, I knew he'd be able to do this quickly because he knew everything about sharks. I just wanted to show him he was *able* to know an answer and raise his hand.

At the end of the year, the teacher emailed me. "I never realized how smart Roger was," she wrote. "He didn't talk until the end of the year, and now I see that he knew most of the answers all along."

Slow processing speed is very common among students who struggle with attention issues and learning challenges. You can spot slow processing speed if your child is taking time to get organized for the next activity, can't organize their thoughts quickly enough to answer a question you or the teacher asks, or seems daydreamy, unmotivated, or just lazy. Even if your child takes some time processing, they are not lazy. They are still as intelligent as the next student.

Slow processing speed is tough for students. New information comes through every day in school. Here are some signs:

- If the teacher gives oral directions, the slow processing child will miss some of them.

- If they are given directions with more than three steps—read, comprehend, and then write about _____—it is very difficult to do all three.

- If they are given a reading assignment, they may not be able to quickly decode some of the words as they read. They then get frustrated and skip words. Or they stop to decode the word and lose the overall meaning of what they're reading.

- If they take a test, they may know the material but aren't able to read, write, and finish the test in the time given.

- If they have to transition from one activity to another, it can be difficult for them to gather their things together and get ready. This includes getting organized for school and going to bed.

- If they are in social situations, they can have a hard time staying in the loop in terms of social interaction and keeping up with peer conversations.

While you can almost always spot slow processing, it is clinically measured on professionally administered tests that tell how fast a child processes new information. If medication is suggested, you will want to take your child to a psychiatrist who can prescribe the meds and then see your child frequently to make sure the medicine is working. Getting the right medication can help your child stay focused so that they can decode words while they are reading and stay on task.

After Alex was tested and began taking medication, I noticed a marked difference in his decoding skills. "Alex," I told him, "I am so pleased that you are stopping at unknown words and using your decoding skills."

"Really, Vicki," he replied. "Did you think for all those months I wasn't listening to you teach me about blends, digraphs, vowels, suffixes, and prefixes? I was listening, but my brain couldn't take it all in and then decode all those words I didn't know."

> Getting the right medication can help your child stay focused so they can decode words while reading and stay on task.

Alex had been trying to get his brain to process all the information I was trying to teach him. He was listening, he just couldn't access it. Now, on medication, he was more attentive and was able to use his decoding skills because his processing speed had improved.

Meds help but don't solve the problem. Even if a child is on medication, their writing and spelling can remain impacted until they learn word analysis skills and are successful at using the computer. Students who are helped by medication may also need some help gaining confidence about speaking in front of the class. And they still need an educational specialist. The educational specialist can create study sheets and help your child organize the work that needs to be studied.

HELPFUL ACCOMMODATIONS

Certain accommodations made for your child by their teachers, including sitting up front to focus better, are helpful. Teachers should also be communicating with you and other educators about the schoolwork coming up. Make sure the teacher gives you and the educational specialist a sense of what they are studying and what bigger reports, tests, and reading are on the horizon. Read and discuss the assigned books that the teacher is having your child read. Hiring an educational specialist to work with your child, along with giving them medication, if needed, can prevent outbursts and other emotional reactions.

Anyone working with a child, including teachers and outside educators, should be working toward the student's passions and strengths. If they are interested in doing what they love, their response time is faster. If they play sports they love, they are better at processing directions from the coach, and this can be practice for following directions in school.

Al's dad is a "jock." Al is dreadful at sports, but his dad said he had to do football. The child cried telling me about it. He never listens when he's at football practice, is awful at it, and hates doing it. I suggested other classes to the dad, but he was intent on Al being just like him, a jock. No wonder Al doesn't pay attention.

No matter what they are involved in, children also need to know that it's okay to ask for help. My student Monica, who is 28 now and studying to be a lawyer, said she asked every teacher to help with tests from high school on. By having tests given orally or by taking them on computer, she received better grades. She said teachers were very nice about accommodating her.

And, of course, medication doesn't mean children hear you when you call them five times. Try not to get upset when your child is late. Instead, begin communicating with them about preparation ahead of time. For instance, you might have to lay out their clothes for school the night before and get them up a few minutes earlier than you think you need to, so that they have time to get ready.

Children who process slower than those around them can feel like the world is going too fast, and they can't catch up. Watch out for signs of overwhelm and high frustration levels. Try to work with your child's teachers and educational specialist by asking them to take the following actions:

- Sit the child up front.

- Give extra time on tests.

- Make sure your child has enough time to answer questions before going on to the next child.

- If students write homework in their planners, ask the teacher to check that your child has their homework written down. Some of my students have a homework planner but don't write anything in it.

- After giving directions, ask the teacher to check if your child understands what to do. This can be done by walking by the desk and quietly asking your child to repeat what is to be done.

- When a project is assigned, show some examples.

Recognizing that a child has slow processing speed is the first step in helping them. Some children may benefit from medication; for others, simply making sure that teachers and relevant others are aware of your child's particular learning differences may be enough. Children who process information differently are sometimes miscategorized as lazy or "just not listening." With the right information, the professionals who interact with your child can account for the fact that some kids just do things at a different pace.

SENSORY PROCESSING

Some of my students have sensory processing issues. Sensory processing is about all the sensory systems working together. The sensory systems are hearing, visual, tactile (touch), smell, taste, and two systems that aren't familiar to everyone, proprioceptive and vestibular. Proprioceptive is the body in relation to the environment. This may be an issue if your child breaks pencils a lot, can't grade their movement correctly, or slams a door. The child might push, hit, or grab at things or people.

The vestibular system has to do with head position, spatial orientation, and motion. It involves the inner circular canals in the ear, motor function, balance, and posture. You might notice your child falls out of his chair or jumps around and spins a lot. These two systems, proprioceptive and vestibular, work together.

Does your child have:

- Sensitivity to sounds . . . if something is loud, do they place their hands over their ears?

- Sensitivity to the way clothes feel?

- Sensitivity to the tastes or smells of foods, or to foods that touch each other on their plate?

- Sensitivity to touch?

- Sensitivity to various lighting within a room?

- Trouble focusing because they're distracted by many things?

- Undersensitivity? Does your child need to touch everything around them? Does your child get in the way of others' space or take risks?

As a parent you can monitor your child because you know what bothers them. Share your knowledge with the teacher and give them ideas to help your child. Have the teacher seat your child away from anything distracting and maybe put a cushion on their seat.

At home, when doing homework, have your child wear earphones to help with their sensitivity to noises. Let them choose what clothes they want to wear that feel good on them. In social situations, like birthday parties, prepare them ahead so you can help if they become overwhelmed with the noise or number of people there. If they are sensitive to heat or cold, be sure to watch them, especially near the stove or any other dangers.

AUDITORY PROCESSING

If your child has a deficit in auditory processing, they can hear sounds but can't decipher which sound is which. I give a test where I show pictures of two things that sound the same—for example, *man-van*. Then I ask the child to pick out the van. I can see if they hear the difference between the sounds of man and van. In oral directions and asking questions about what was read, if they can't distinguish sounds, they may not be able to understand what you want them to do. Of course, children with speech issues may have this issue, too. Your team should include a speech and language professional and maybe a hearing doctor (audiologist) to make sure your child has no hearing issues. But one thing to remember is you must find out if this is a hearing, speech, or even attention issue.

If your child has any of these issues, they would appear on the full battery of tests the professional gives your child.

VISUAL PROCESSING

Visual processing is making sense of information taken in through the eyes. The brain of a child who is having difficulty with visual processing doesn't properly receive and read cues sent by the eyes. Visual processing issues are different from vision issues, which have to be checked by an ophthalmologist.

Many of the symptoms of visual processing issues are similar to those of attention issues. If your child doesn't pay attention in class, is easily distracted, reverses letters in words or math numbers, has writing issues, or does not do well with comprehension after they've read or listened to a teacher in class, they could be diagnosed as having visual processing issues or attention issues. It's a fine line.

Eight Types of Visual Processing Issues

Visual Discrimination Issues
When your child has trouble seeing differences between similar letters, shapes, or objects.

Visual Figure-Ground Discrimination Issues
Your child struggles to distinguish a shape or letter from its background.

Visual Sequencing Issues
They have difficulty seeing shapes, letters, or words in the correct order, and they may skip lines.

Visual Motor Processing Issues
They can't write on lines or copy from a book.
They might also walk into things.

Long- or Short-Term Memory Issues
If they can't remember shapes, they may have issues with reading and spelling.

Visual-Closure Issues

They can see only part of an object.

Letter and Symbol Reversal Issues

They switch or confuse visually similar letters or numbers, like *b* and *d*.

Visual Spatial Issues

They can't tell how far things are from one another.

THE TAKEAWAY

Processing differences can look like other issues in some students, depending on the individual child and the challenges they may be facing. A teacher may believe a child with slow processing speed is lazy or doesn't listen well, children with sensory process differences can seem restless, and so forth. The right diagnosis and accommodations can make a world of difference for these students.

What has to be remembered is *not* what your child *can't* do but what they *can* do. A test administered by a professional will give you the answers. It's not what the issues are called that is the most important, but how the knowledge of those issues is used by a trained professional to teach your child.

[13]

Is There a Best School for My Child?

Michael Phelps is a competitive swimmer and the most successful and decorated Olympian of all time. He has learning differences, yet he holds the record for the most Olympic medals won by an athlete: 23 gold medals, 3 silver, and 2 bronze. He said he had a teacher tell him that he would never amount to anything and would never be successful. Ideally, you'll find a school where teachers *encourage* your child.

———————————— // ————————————

There is no list of the best schools for your child, but you want a school with teachers and administrators who will understand your child with learning differences, accommodate them in the classroom, and work with outside therapists to help find ways to teach your child.

THE LATE-NIGHT EMAILS

I work late at night because I like the quiet of the house at that hour. Sitting at my desk, I can see the moonlight shining through the 100-foot grevillea (silk oak) tree outside my window. My white Labrador, Tutor, sits under my desk at my feet. It's midnight. I hear a ping. A new email from a parent.

Many years ago, before the internet, I communicated with parents by phone. If I was teaching at a school, there were parent-teacher conferences about each child. Now, as an educational specialist in private practice, I receive emails from parents, teachers, and principals. But the late-night ones are different from the daytime emails that might just be sent to confirm times for therapy.

Concerns, fears, and frustrations about a child's ability to succeed in school fill these late-night emails. They contain teacher, testing, or family questions that start with: "What do I do?" Usually, the letters are from a parent asking why the school can't help more, why they have to pay all this money for outside therapy, why a teacher doesn't understand the child, or what to do if a teacher treats the child unfairly. Parents talk about the battery of tests that don't demonstrate to the school their child's true abilities. The parents are almost always unsure about the best way to help their child.

One particular evening, I received three emails from Patti. The subject box had her son's name and an unhappy face next to it. Her son, Jake, was eight years old and attending a new private school for students with learning differences. Patti stated in her first email that Jake had been given a battery of reading assessments and received below the first percentile on every test. Next to the percentile it said in bold letters, "Very Poor."

In the next two emails, she for-warded emails from the head admin-istrator of the school containing *six* pages of negative comments. Really, all negative comments? Did any-body at that school ever learn to say positive remarks about a student?

Don't always take negative test results at face value. Factors beyond your child's control may affect their performance.

"He seems brighter than this," Patti wrote to me.

I had been working with Jake for a year. He could read, but he had slow processing speed and they had given him a timed test. The time aspect had penalized him for his slow reading, and it was not an accurate measurement of his *actual* reading.

"When was this test given?" I asked when I wrote Patti back.

"Three weeks ago."

WHAT WENT WRONG

I was shocked. Then angry. Those were the weeks Jake's doc-tor had taken him off medication for ADHD, when he was trying to figure out why it was having such an adverse effect on Jake, and he'd been waiting to try another one. The school, knowing he was off medication, had given him several bat-teries of reading tests. I was surprised he even scored first percentile. I wondered why the school hadn't waited until Jake was on medication again.

Patti explained that she had indeed told the school about Jake being off medication, but they said that was when the tests were being given, so he had to take them. Here was a new private school for students with learning differences, and they were giving a child with ADHD assessment tests while he wasn't on medication. The tests had no validity.

> No school is perfect, but one may be markedly better for *your* child. And the same applies to teachers.

Jake had been asked to leave his public school because they couldn't accommodate his learning. But teachers at this new school were not well trained to work with different learners, even though they said they were. Now Patti was afraid to say anything to the teachers because she wasn't sure where Jake would go if she upset the educators at this school.

Two weeks later, when he was on his new medication, I tested Jake with an untimed reading test, and he read at a second-grade level and scored 100% on comprehension.

Thinking about this now makes me so sad. Luckily, Jake switched schools after that. Now he is at a private school with many great teachers who help him, accommodate him in the classroom, and work well with me. No school is perfect, but one may be better for your child than another. And one teacher may be better than another.

Another late-night email came about David, a first grader I had been working with. David is the one who had walked into my house holding three *Titanic* books. "I want to learn everything there is about the *Titanic*." For eight months David's sessions with me were all about the *Titanic*. He wrote about it, learned vocabulary from it, and was able to gain all the skills he needed to learn how to read.

But one fateful night at 12:30 a.m., I received an email from Janie, David's mom: "David loves what you are doing with the *Titanic*. He's so into it and reading up a storm. But today he came home from school and told me the teacher, Mrs. Fider, announced they are having a Literary Tea and each student could come dressed as their favorite character from a book. And then he started crying and said, 'Mrs. Fider told us about the tea, and then, in front of the class, she told me not to come dressed in anything from the *Titanic*. Now I have to choose another book.'"

SOME TEACHERS ARE JUST INFLEXIBLE

I knew this teacher. I had been the reading specialist in her school, and she had taught the same way for 20 years. She wanted her room quiet and boring. She yelled at any child who didn't sit quietly in their seat. Her tone even scared me, and I disliked how she treated students with learning differences.

Janie knew that if she talked to the principal or the teacher, she risked Mrs. Fider being mean to her child the rest of the year. A parent of a child with learning differences is often afraid to talk to the teacher and the administrators for fear their child will be asked to leave the school, or the teacher will be mean to their child.

Janie chose a solution that protected her child from future mean looks or sarcastic comments: she kept David home from school on Literary Tea Day.

If Janie had asked me to, I could have handled the situation. I was working in close contact with the teacher. She was not an easy person to deal with, but I don't think she would have reacted to me the same way she would have reacted to Janie. Mrs. Fider is still teaching and I still hear negative stories about her.

In the 1980s I read an article about Tony Baxter, who was, at that time, the senior vice-president of creative development at Walt Disney Imagineering. He was responsible for creating designs and in charge of construction of many attractions in the Disneyland parks. He oversaw Big Thunder Mountain Railroad, Star Tours, and Splash Mountain.

My students chose to study all about the imagineers at Disney and then built rides out of junk based on the themes of their books.

Splash Mountain was just about to open, so I called Tony. He agreed to meet my students at Disney and talk about the imagineers and then show us the actual rides being constructed there. Then he arranged for my students to go on Splash Mountain before it opened to the public.

Every executive function was used during this unit I created. And not one child complained or was bored! I bet every city in the country has something interesting that your child or students would like.

I have always chosen schools to teach at that allow me to do projects using the passions and strengths of my students. I realize you can't always choose a school to send your child to, or choose teachers for them to have, but if they are under-stimulated, you can find someone in your area who would be great for your child to meet. In all my years teaching, no one has ever turned me down. Most people, when they hear you have a child or are a teacher of students with learning differences, are glad to help.

THE TAKEAWAY

The best teachers—whether in public or private schools, or in special schools for students with learning differences—are the ones who really care about teaching *every child* and accept every child for who they are. Most teachers in public or private schools probably had only one class in college about learning differences and were likely not taught specifically how to work with children with learning differences. Some are open to learning the best methods for teaching a child with learning differences and even go to workshops and take classes at night. The educational specialist on your team can work closely with the teacher, helping with ideas for teaching your child.

Teachers, test scores, and insensitive administrators have an impact on the success or failure of your child. And remember, not all your children may do well at the same school. You, as the primary advocate for your child, must be on top of what's going on at your child's school. Children know when someone isn't treating them fairly or someone is being mean to them. Always remember to listen to your child, then talk with the educational specialist you use and decide on a plan to work better with the professionals at the school.

[14]

Your Child's
Passions and Strengths

Astronaut Scott Kelly has said, "I was able to operate pretty well on the International Space Station and I think one of the things that helped me, maybe because I have a little bit of an attention issue, was I was really good at focusing on the stuff that was really important and not letting all other distracting details take away from my attention, or affect my ability to do the important things well."

———————————— // ————————————

What I realize from all my years of experience and travel is that you can't really know what a child is capable of unless you ask them about their passions. Talent and brain power are often hidden in the child's interest.

Wherever I go, I run into someone who has learning differences. When I walked into the library at Trinity College in Dublin with its 200,000 books from the 15th century, I had a feeling that somewhere in this trove of books existed information about children who learned differently, even back in the early centuries.

THE "NO-HOPERS" CLASS

I saw a man wearing a name tag, and I thought he might have my answer. Lawrence was retired, about 5 feet tall with a warm smile. He was one of those students I was asking about. "I was in the 'no-hopers' class," he said. "Because there was no hope for us. The only person who believed in me was my mom. For years, she was the one who got me all the help I needed."

"Did you have any passions?" I asked. I was always interested in what smart children were interested in and always surprised at the answers.

He nodded. "Trucks. Loved trucks and still do. My mom took me to truck shows, bought me trucks for every holiday, and I built them out of any materials I could find." He laughed.

Lawrence eventually became the CEO of a huge trucking company. Anytime he wanted to, he could drive a really big truck. "I did go back to my awful teacher," Lawrence said. "And he didn't remember me. I told him how dreadful he was to me, how he thought there was no hope for me. Then I told him how smart I really was and handed him my business card with my name and title as president of my trucking company and walked away." Lawrence had followed his passion to incredible success.

Not long after I met Lawrence, I was on a boat in Italy. The waiter asked what I did. When I told him, he told me about the tests his child had been given by a neuropsychologist and what the results were. I asked about his son's passions or strengths, and he told me his son was the youngest pianist in his hometown outside Istanbul, Turkey. He was already playing in piano concerts at eight years old.

No matter where in the world you are, students who learn differently have passions. If you ask the right questions and dig into their interests enough, you will find that they have something they do unbelievably well.

> If your child loves what they're doing, they can often focus much more intently than when they're bored or uninterested.

Most parents don't understand how their child can focus for hours playing the piano but can't focus for 10 minutes on a math worksheet. If your child loves something, the focus often comes. That's why parents, educators, and educational specialists teach most effectively when they integrate the child's passions into their lessons.

I gave the waiter on the boat hope that he indeed had a special son. We also talked about how, with the right interventions, the child would succeed. We talked about finding a psychiatrist to discuss medication for his son. But most important, I told him to keep promoting his son's incredible talent.

We've talked about using a child's passion to address their slow processing speed and to teach them reading, writing, and executive functioning, but it can often be good to simply dive into a student's passions without a set agenda and give them real-life experiences doing what they love. What arises from simply engaging them in what they love can change the trajectory of their lives forever.

GETTING OUTSIDE YOUR COMFORT ZONE

You do need a little courage to do this for your child! A few days ago, my seven-year-old student Lucy and I were driving in the car when I stopped to ask a woman where she bought her Labrador retriever, because my 15-year-old lab was dying. After I got the information, Lucy said, "Why do you always talk to random people?" Hilarious coming from a seven-year-old! Until that moment I had never thought about my quirky trait of talking to everyone. If I meet someone here in Los Angeles, or any part of the world, who works in a field that is of interest to one of my students, I have no trouble asking if I could contact them about doing a project with us. If I can connect my student to them, I can use this to motivate my student to learn to read and write.

I try to contact people who have had learning differences growing up and are now very successful. The reaction from my students is always, "If this person succeeded, maybe I can succeed, too."

The best part of the experience is when my students go back to their class and report on the event. Many of my students never talk in class, but after one of these incredible experiences, they go to class and show pictures and feel special. What a confidence builder!

Most of the time, if you have a child with learning differences, people are very nice and will try to accommodate you. If you read a story about a person your child might be interested in, you can email or call that person's office. You may not be able to visit, but most people will at least respond if you write to them. I have never called or emailed a person for a student and gotten no for an answer.

"YOU HAVE TO LOVE WHAT YOU DO"

I taught twin boys who loved the competitive eater Joey Chestnut. Joey is mainly famous for winning the hot dog challenge that Nathan's Famous Hot Dogs in New York holds each year. In 2020 Joey won by eating 75 hot dogs and buns in 10 minutes. When researching Joey, the boys were shocked at how many other contests he had won, including eating 141 hardboiled eggs in 8 minutes, 257 Hostess Donuts in 6 minutes, and even 54 cow brain tacos in eight minutes! (He didn't like those!) I emailed Joey and asked, because of COVID, if he'd do a Zoom with the boys. The boys researched every contest Joey entered, wrote questions for him, and interviewed him. I think it was the only Zoom during COVID they loved! Joey answered their questions, saying he had been in over 300 contests, was usually tired after a contest, doesn't usually get sick after a contest, and, yes, does poop more than usual for the next couple of days after a contest! (Their favorite answer!)

But Joey's closing words were the most important: "You have to love what you do and I do." Wise words from a hero to many children.

My student, Casey, could tell you the names of every exotic car ever made, when it was made, and how many were made. He is an encyclopedia of cars. We took field trips to exotic car dealerships, and he got to sit in every car. On weekends, his dad took him to car shows. Then, using incredible executive functioning skills, he went into my garage and created a magnificent car out of junk!

After that, he sat down and used fantastic writing and storytelling skills to write a whole story about his car, how it was the first of its kind, the colors it came in, its speed, size, and how much it will cost. He didn't have to practice his spelling words. He learned how to write and spell by focusing on a subject he was interested in.

MAKING ALMOST ANYTHING INTERESTING

Casey picked Oklahoma out of a hat in his classroom for his state report. When I heard I said, "Really? I don't know anything about Oklahoma?" I got out *The 50 States* by Gabrielle Balkan, which, I think, is the best state book for kids. We turned to Oklahoma and learned there was the most amazing car museum with unusual, incredible model cars built in the last 60 years by Darryl Starbird. Of course, we called Mr. Starbird, and he sent Casey a fabulous book with pictures of all his cars and his wonderful story. Afterward, we went to Google for more information on Oklahoma and found out something else that was interesting about Oklahoma. The process of fracking had caused Oklahoma to have hundreds of earthquakes a year. Fascinating! Reading the book and using Google made this an engaging assignment for a smart boy.

> Some things to think about:
>
> • Assigned school subjects are not usually what students are interested in, but parents and educational therapists can help a child research and find their hidden passions in such classroom assignments.
>
> • Children are always good at something. They know they are with me for a reason related to what they cannot do. That is why I find what they *can* do and use it to teach what they can't do.
>
> • Encouraging a child's strengths in one non-academic area can make all the difference to the way the child feels in school when they are having difficulties in learning.

ENCOURAGEMENT FROM AN EXPERT

I started seeing Rory when he was in second grade. He had many learning differences and his dad refused to have him tested. His teacher was mean to him because she thought he was lazy and disrespectful to her. I worked with Rory in school in my reading center and also privately. We both loved antiques, and he loved and collected Hot Wheels toy cars.

One day when I was reading the *Los Angeles Times*, I found an article on a man named Jim who was head of the design team at Mattel in charge of Hot Wheels and Matchbox cars. When the designer was interviewed, he sounded just like Rory! He had been bored in school, couldn't sit still, liked to build, collected Matchbox cars, and was not a good student. I immediately called him.

I talked to Jim and convinced him to allow Rory to interview him at Mattel. It turned out to be the turning point in Rory's development. He had to research Hot Wheels and write questions for the interview. He had a lot of questions about certain cars because he collected them.

The day came for our trip. From the moment Jim met us at the door, I had no idea what he and Rory were talking about. There were glass-enclosed cases with Mattel toy vintage cars in them that they talked about at length. I had never seen Rory so animated and happy! He told Jim he wanted to do exactly what Jim did when he grew up.

"Take it from me," Jim told Rory when he said goodbye. "I nearly screwed up my whole life because I wasn't concentrating in school. I had to work six times harder to make up." He squatted down and looked Rory in the eye. "If you want to design Matchbox cars, you have to know how to do math, design the cars, write up what you want to make, and present your ideas aloud to people. So, you'd better start concentrating in school," he said. "And working really hard. You sound like a smart kid, and you're a lot like me. It took me time to get my act together, but thankfully, I did because I love every day that I come to work here."

Rory had a great year. When he was tested, he was found to have learning differences and ADHD. He continued working with me until middle school. Rory recently emailed me to tell me how as an eighth grader he designed an invention for a security device for his school science project, won first prize, and has applied for a patent for the product.

AN AMAZING FIELD TRIP

In 2016 I had five boys in second and third grades with learning differences who loved outer space. Astronaut Scott Kelly was in space for a year that year, so we watched YouTubes of him each time they came to me. We read about space and researched and wrote about space. I taught all decoding skills using space words. They were as mesmerized as I was. Of course, my students talked about how Scott Kelly took his urine and recycled it and made it into drinking water. From researching we also found out Scott had learning differences in school.

I attended a student evaluation meeting with a neuropsychologist named Karen and heard her talking about her husband, who worked as a rocket scientist making spacecraft at Elon Musk's SpaceX. Since the factory was right here in the Los Angeles area, I immediately asked if SpaceX had tours. Karen said they did but only for family and friends. Karen was nice enough to set up a tour for my students to SpaceX to see Elon Musk's spacecraft being made. My students continued studying about Scott Kelly and looked up everything about Elon Musk. They wrote questions for Karen's husband to ask when we met him. Each student also made a spacecraft out of the art supplies and junk I had in my garage.

It was an amazing day, seeing the actual spacecrafts being made before our eyes and learning all about them from Karen's husband. He was very patient and answered all the wonderful questions the boys asked. My students wrote thank-you letters. Roger wrote, "Thank you for showing me the spacecrafts. The lemonade was good, too." And truthfully, what a combination: spacecrafts and lemonade.

> **Not every important improvement shows up on a test. Self-confidence can be its own reward.**

The rocket scientist wrote back to the students that they had bright, curious minds and their journey from discussing to creating their own spacecraft was so inspiring to him because that's what learning is all about.

My students wrote reports about their trip to SpaceX and included facts about Scott Kelly being in space. Then they not only showed the spacecrafts they made—which, by the way, were incredible—but presented a report to their class. Even the teachers were impressed, especially that the students got up in front of the class, read, and told about such an incredible journey they had.

The teachers told me they saw a difference in the children after that. They seemed to have more confidence and were more willing to share in class discussions. And there was a difference in the attitudes of the other students. They were enthralled with the story that my students had gotten to see the real spacecrafts that Elon Musk was making. Sometimes growth isn't shown on a test. It is shown in actions and attitudes that change when students gain confidence.

When I met children's book authors at national reading conventions in the 1980s and '90s, I always invited them to visit my school. Luckily, it didn't cost that much and my school paid for the author to visit. I'd have my students be the hosts and hostesses when the famous author came. During the visit, the students performed for the author. Our favorite book one year was Nina Laden's *The Night I Followed the Dog*, about a boy who follows his dog and finds out that at night the dog gets into a tuxedo, sneaks out into a limo, and goes to a club for dogs. Three-fourths of my students loved singing, acting, dancing, and writing scripts. *Mamma Mia!* was a hit musical and the songs were being sung by literally every student I taught. We had the idea of a play as our culminating activity of the year. The students wrote a script based on *The Night I Followed the Dog*, dressed in fabulous dog costumes made by the parents, and rewrote the entire book in songs with the tunes from *Mamma Mia!*

FINDING THE RIGHT WORDS

I had a student, Shaun, who spoke only when called upon. Everyone thought he was not intelligent. But I felt differently. His family spoke only Farsi at home, and I felt he was smart but didn't have the English words to express himself aloud. He talked to me but never talked in class in front of other students. One day he came to me and asked if he could bring his guitar to play the music in our play.

I had no idea he played the guitar, but I thought it was fine if he brought it. My colleague thought I was crazy to let a child who never spoke bring his guitar: "What if he can't play?" This wasn't Broadway after all, I thought. "He can strum, I'm sure," I answered.

Not only did Shaun bring his guitar, but he had learned all the songs and sat on the edge of the stage and played throughout the entire play. In her thank you to the group, Nina Laden ended with a big thank you to the best dog guitarist she'd ever met. One person's words just may change a child forever.

In April of 2016 I bumped into Shaun's mom at the farmers' market. I was so excited to hear about how he was doing. She pulled out a picture of a handsome man, 24 years old, now living in Boston and finishing his master's degree in business.

"That show changed his life forever. He was so proud. I think because we spoke only Farsi at home, he just didn't have the command of the English language. He was shy, and everyone, except you, thought he was dumb. He is very successful today."

THE TAKEAWAY

The children I have taught *are* interested in learning. The key to unlocking their wealth of knowledge lies in accessing their passions. Everyone should be working together as a team, using a child's passions and strengths. When you find a way to engage a child, they can learn to read and write and become happy. The key is there if you look hard enough and work with the child on the basis of what they can do, not what they can't do.

[15]

Helping to Build Confidence in Your Child

Henry Winkler, actor, director, producer, and children's book author, has learning differences. He has stated, "This is what I know: a learning challenge doesn't have to stop you. Your learning challenge will not stop you from meeting your dream. Only you will stop yourself from meeting your dream."

———————— // ————————

There are many ways to help build confidence in your child and help them with their feelings about learning. "Think about Alex," I emailed Alex's six therapists one night. "For so long he's had to go to outside help for learning, has been separated from his class for reading, has felt behind socially, and can't seem to catch up. How does he feel?"

We'd been talking about Alex because he had started compulsively pulling his hair out. Students who are facing learning differences have an increased level of anxiety and lower confidence, and it's easy to understand why. My dissertation thesis research was an ethnographic study observing teachers in elementary schools in the Cincinnati, Ohio, area to determine if they talked differently to their high and low readers. For part of the research, I observed teachers teaching reading to groups of different reading levels. Then I interviewed the students about their thoughts on how they read.

"WHAT IF I NEVER LEARN?"

I began by interviewing 15 five-year-old kindergarten students. I'd take one child at a time into the hall. All they had been told was that I was going to ask them about reading. We sat on two small chairs across from one another. I would ask each child, "Can you read?" Then, I would ask, "Who in your class is able to read, and who can't?" This was the second month of school. These children had just met their classmates for the first time, and all 15 of them were able to tell me which reading group they were in. Each student also understood that there were two reading groups and that one group of children could read and one group could not.

The children in the nonreading group spoke anxiously about their fear of never learning to read. They said the readers were smart, but they were not. They were already asking this very scary question: What if I never learn?

Signs of stress showed up in their behavior in the classroom. Children in the higher group raised their hand to answer questions, freely asked questions, and were confident about reading aloud words on the board. The nonreaders sat playing with their pencils, looking around, and never raised their hands.

Fast-forward to first, second, and third grades. Children with learning differences continue to experience higher stress and greater challenges in class. During these grades, the anxiety about not reading, and maybe not writing, gets multiplied as more students learn to read and write. "Will I ever learn? Am I dumb?" these students wonder. "Everyone is smarter than me," they think. "Everyone has better attention than me." When the teacher calls on them, they freeze. They often wonder why they have to work so hard and yet never finish their work on time. One of their biggest questions is: "What's wrong with me?"

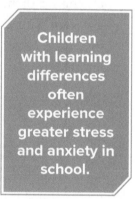

Children with learning differences often experience greater stress and anxiety in school.

Frequently, schools have a "pull-out class" for students who are having difficulty learning to read. Having to be pulled out of class brings up horrific anxiety and worry. The child becomes unhappy and embarrassed about not being able to read. They keep hearing everyone say they are smart, and they think, "If I am smart, why can't I read, write, or pay attention?"

You can see how their confidence would start to suffer, and they would have trouble with anxiety.

How do you help with your child's anxiety? How do you ensure that their confidence stays strong, that they will be able to read with the proper tools, and that there is nothing actually *wrong* with them?

The team of professionals helping your child can be pivotal to your child's confidence. When you have good communication between you, the teachers, and the therapists, you will get a sense of whether your child might be moving into overwhelm—tantrums, compulsive behavior, crying jags, and so on. It's traumatic for a child to be behind his or her peers in reading and writing. It can be devastating and terribly embarrassing for them to feel separate and "less than" their peers. Working with a team, you can prepare a student for when they have to get in front of a class, which can bring on an inordinate amount of stress and anxiety for a child, especially a child with a speech issue. They can practice reading their reports to a member of the team beforehand, for example.

Because I know these students can have anxiety and stress, I make my room the safe room. All feelings can be expressed, and I can help the students communicate with their parents if needed. If you find that conflicted emotions continue to persist, despite the team's efforts, it's important that your team includes a professional counselor for the child. That way, if a report is due, or a test or a performance is coming up, or something happens socially and they experience meltdowns, you can rely on this therapist to help.

THE GROWTH MINDSET

Carol Dweck developed a concept of Growth Mindset at Stanford University. She studied why some people succeed and some don't and how we have the power within to be successful. She found that a child's view of himself can determine everything. If a child has a fixed mindset, their qualities often can't be changed. They have trouble with challenges. They may give up. They are who they are.

The child with a growth mindset has the gumption to "stick to it." These children thrive during challenging times by having the resilience and perseverance to carry on. For parents and educators of students with differences, this is very important. Don't praise the child's intelligence or talent, praise their work, their effort, their strategies, their focus, how they approached the problem, and their improvement. Hopefully, this will get them from the fixed mindset to a growth mindset. A growth mindset for children struggling in school is extremely important.

> Some ideas for activities outside school that can build your child's growth mindset:
>
> • Enrolling your child in an after-school class where they are meeting children from other schools can build their confidence. After-school activities stimulate them in directions that are not necessarily academic but can still teach them skills and relax them. After-school activities help children expand friendships and take them away from the educational identity that plagues them.
>
> • If your child likes building, try out a LEGO class.
>
> • If they love sports, make sure they get their choice of which sport to engage in. Music, art, cooking, gymnastics, and karate can all help

your child feel included in a group activity and build the confidence they need.

- Building friendships is important to countering anxiety. Even if your child seems to have only one good friend, make sure they get together outside school. One good friend is important! Sometimes that good friend is a cousin, a friend from an outside class, or a friend made at summer camp. No matter who that friend is or where they are from, make an effort to get them together.

- Pets can be a huge boon to your child's well-being. You can involve pets in helping to hone skills they will need for school. For instance, Alex gave my dog Carat a Bark Mitzvah and then decided to do a Hamstermitzvah for his hamster, Gerald. An enormous amount of executive functioning went into the planning: making the invitations, creating decorations, designing a menu, scheduling activities, and making a crossword puzzle of hamster facts for his friends. Alex wrote a haiku poem about Gerald and called it Hamsterku, like the book *Dogku*. And he made Gerald a chair and table out of clay. He made the chocolate cake hamsters out of an Easter egg mold, decorating them with licorice whiskers, M&M eyes, and frosting. He bought Gerald a little doll's bow tie and made it fit around his neck. Then he took remote control cars, glued little seats to them, and put the hamster cakes on the cars.

The Hamstermitzvah improved Alex's social life. When the children came over, they raced the hamster cars across Alex's living room, making sure not to hit the furniture and get the frosting all over the place. The Hamstermitzvah was a success, but unfortunately, Gerald, who is nocturnal, fell asleep on top of his table 10 minutes into the party and missed the whole thing. Believe me, Gerald was the talk of school the next day and Alex was feeling more confident and more social because of the party he organized.

DEALING WITH A BULLY

Finding situations where your child can socialize is key because bullying can sometimes be a problem for children with learning differences. Knowing how to deal with that can be touchy. Ollie, a fourth grader I was working with, was 5 feet 8 inches tall, loved basketball, and was constantly being bullied by Will, another student in his class, who taunted him all day long. Will called Ollie "big and dumb," bumped into him when he walked by, and pushed him so he'd drop the basketball. He'd also reach out and grab whatever Ollie was holding.

Every session, Ollie complained about Will. "If you're 5 feet 8," I said to him, "how tall is Will? He must be really tall!" But Ollie shook his head. "He's short, around 5 feet 2." I widened my eyes in shock. "And does he make baskets like you do?" Ollie shook his head. A short bully was pushing around my tall student, who could play basketball. But because of his lack of confidence, Ollie was being picked on.

Of course, I gave him the usual suggestions: report him to the teacher; remember that anyone who bullies is a sad, unhappy person; and last, just ignore him. But these suggestions border on cliché, and they actually don't work that well if a child lacks confidence.

Knowing Ollie was good at basketball, I kept up with the different teams. He knew every statistic about every basketball team, and we read and wrote about them. Then one day I read about the 7-foot 6-inch basketball player from Senegal, Mamadou N'Diaye, who played at UC Irvine. I called the basketball office at UC Irvine and asked if Ollie and I could come to a game. Not only did they say yes, but they invited Ollie to be a ball boy! What an incredible experience for Ollie.

On Monday morning, he told his class about his adventures. This experience gave him a tremendous amount of confidence. After that, he was actually able to ignore the bully, not showing any reaction at all when Will tried his usual antics.

There are other activities outside school to build your child's confidence, like Ollie's visit to the basketball game.

- Newspapers sometimes have contests that your child can enter. The *Los Angeles Times* had a Halloween contest and my students made pop-up Halloween pictures with stories to go with them and won! My student Kenny, who showed up on my doorstep years after I had worked with him and had completed a master's degree in environmental science (MESc) from Yale, a master's of arts in geography (MA) from Clark, and a PhD in geography, carried a newspaper clipping he'd cut out after he won the paper's Halloween contest in 1994! It had been under the glass on his desktop for 23 years. Back when no one except me and his mom believed in him, he was blown away that he'd won the contest, and it boosted how he felt about himself.

- Grace, a fifth-grade student, always enters contests. She created a candy heart with the saying "PUGS AND KISSES" for the Necco Company, which makes Valentine's Sweethearts. The company had been in business since 1866 and sells 8 billion Sweethearts a year on Valentine's Day. Grace's saying won the contest, and every box of Sweethearts came with her saying on the heart candies. Think about your child taking their winning candy to school!

- Mike Thaler, author of over 200 humorous short chapter books in the *Black Lagoon* series (which my students love), now writes emails that you can sign up to receive. Near Halloween he asked for kids to send in their jokes. Three of my students had their jokes published in his newsletter. The email went out to thousands of children. My students took the email to school for show-and-tell. All the other kids in class surrounded them to catch a glimpse of the email.

- To enter your child in a contest, look under "contests for kids" on Google. *National Geographic* has them all the time. There are writing contests for kids, *Guinness Book of World Records* competitions, art contests, helicopter challenges for airplane enthusiasts, and design-your-own spacecraft contests. Recognize your child's passions and see if there is a contest they can enter.

- The *Los Angeles Times* used to have a kids' corner and children could send in short reviews of books they had read and liked. My kids were in this section all the time. What a thrill to see their work in the newspaper! Unfortunately, the *Times* doesn't do that anymore. Check your local papers to see if they have a kid section or any contests for kids.

- Reach out to accomplished people in the industry your child is interested in and see if you can make an acquaintance. This can absolutely boost your child's confidence outside the classroom.

I met Chris Fallows, one of the foremost authorities and best photographers of sharks in the world, on a boat in South Africa. He was a lecturer on the boat. You can see him each year on the Discovery Channel's *Shark Week* television show. These shows are also on YouTube all the time. I went up to him after one of his lectures and told him how many of my students love sharks and asked if he'd write back to them if they wrote to him with questions about sharks. He agreed!

Every boy I have taught loves sharks! Before we wrote to Chris, they studied everything they could about sharks, read and wrote favorite facts, and watched Chris online. They made sharks out of clay or using the junk stored in my garage. They came up with many questions, wrote to Chris, and Chris wrote back. Then they went to class and stood in front of 30 classmates and read the questions they had written to Chris. They read his answers and showed their projects. I can promise you no one bullied them or made fun of them again. Afterward they told me they were "important" or "famous" in school.

Alex read Kevin Henkes's book *Billy Miller* for a book report and made a shadow box of the story. Since he is very creative, it was spectacular. I had Alex write to Kevin and send a picture of his project. Kevin wrote back and sent a real drawing that he did for Alex of Billy. Alex proudly showed the letter and the drawing from the author to the entire class.

Author visits mean a lot to children. Many author events are on Saturdays, so you can take your child to meet their favorite author. Betty Birney, who writes about a hamster named Humphrey, came to Los Angeles. Alex took Gerald, his hamster, to the presentation and book signing. Then Betty wrote about Alex and his hamster in her blog. Alex was thrilled and shared the blog entry with his class. Not only was it a wonderful day, but Alex had never shared anything in class until he read that blog aloud to his class.

In 2014 a photographer caught a picture of President Obama with a large coin-like object in the palm of his hand. It seemed like he was slipping it to a serviceman like a secret handshake. The caption stated that seeing this exchange was very rare. I was fascinated and looked up the object, which I learned was called a Challenge Coin. Challenge Coins are given out by the president to military or visiting leaders from other countries who have done a good job. These recipients had challenges but had succeeded. Giving the coin to someone is accomplished by slipping the coin into the hand of a deserving person, usually without anyone seeing. Newspaper photographers try to get this exchange but rarely do. June 1, 2014, was the first time in 23 years that a photographer actually got a picture of the exchange.

Twenty years before, I had met a Secret Service agent, Mike, and his girlfriend, who is now his wife, on a plane. I've stayed friends with them and decided to call to see if he knew about this Challenge Coin. Mike, being one of the nicest people I've ever met, said, "Of course, I know about the coin, but the best one in the world is the Challenge Coin given out by the Secret Service. The coin itself is incredible and you cannot buy one like it."

Mike knew I taught children with challenges and how hard they work to succeed.

He then asked, "Would you like me to send you one and set up a time for a Los Angeles agent to present it to your student?"

There was no way I wasn't going to say yes to that incredible offer.

I had shown Alex the picture from the newspaper, and he wanted to know all about the coin. And when I talked to him about Mike, he wanted to learn everything about the Secret Service. Alex had just finished a year working with me six hours a week, plus four hours a week with a speech/language and occupational therapist, not to mention going to regular school, too. If anyone deserved the Challenge Coin it was Alex. That started our journey. We used executive functioning and built self-confidence as we read and studied and wrote questions for the Secret Service agent.

After researching the Secret Service, Alex had many questions to ask. But my three favorites were:

- What do you do when the president goes to the bathroom?

- Would you take a bullet for the president?

- Do you get free sunglasses to wear?

Alex thought the most fascinating fact about the Secret Service was when the Secret Service started. It was established by President Lincoln and the paper had been signed the day before he was shot and killed. So, if someone had tried to kill the president a few weeks later, the president would have been protected by the Secret Service and may not have died.

If you have a child or student who has challenges, works very hard, and is interested in the people who wear black sunglasses and guard the president, you can study about them and then buy one of the replica Challenge Coins from the White House Gift Store online and present it to your child or student. I can assure you it is a confidence builder.

I have been doing this now for many years with the help from my friends in the Secret Service, Mike and Traci, the Secret Service agents who present the coin here in Los Angeles. And this year Mike sent me my own Secret Service Challenge Coin!

THE TAKEAWAY

There is no easy answer to alleviating your child's stress and help them feel good about themselves. But as my students begin to read and see they can learn, I can see their confidence soar. Having therapists and teachers all working together who believe your child *can* learn is of utmost importance. It promotes confidence in your child. It just isn't Mom or Dad saying, "You're smart." It's specialists and teachers believing it, too. Adding in activities that will boost confidence in your child is a priority. Also, it's important to make sure all the professionals on the team work with your child's strengths and passions, and recognize the areas they excel in.

[16]

Technology

Paul Orfalea started Kinko's. He calls his learning differences "learning opportunities." In group projects in school, he would take care of photocopying notes for everyone in order to get out of writing them. He ended up starting the largest photocopy shop in the world. This is just one example of how a child with learning differences finds their passion.

———————— // ————————

The first computer I received was free from BorgWarner in 1971 after I moved to Cincinnati with my new husband, received my master's degree in education with a concentration in the teaching of reading to children with learning differences, and began my career as a reading teacher in an elementary school.

Back then, publishers and other learning companies would give teachers "freebies" to try out in their classrooms. BorgWarner gave me this new machine called a "computer" to try out. The machine stayed in my room until June. My students were mesmerized by it and waited each time for their turn to use it. They wanted to be on it the entire period. I thought the computer could become a great addition to our classroom, but it took away from my teaching and the interaction between students and their interest in actual books. Things are not any different today. Now, according to Common Sense Media, the number of computerized devices in the world surpass the number of people. Ninety-eight percent of children under eight have access to mobile devices. Children 8 to 12 years old spend four to six hours a day with media and technology, and teens up to nine hours a day.

MAKING THE MOST OF SCREEN TIME

What consumes all the children's time on these devices? They are using apps. There are literally millions of apps to choose from. Using the right apps for teaching is an important addition to teaching a child with learning differences. There are educational apps for children with difficulties in reading, writing, math, executive functioning, listening comprehension, social skills, building confidence, and organizing. There are also apps for specific areas like typing, social studies, and science. There are thousands more for practically anything you can think of.

Thoughts before you choose apps for your child:

- What apps cater to my child's passions and strengths?

- What apps will address what my child needs most?

- Where can I try the app?

- Will the teacher or therapist teach me how to do it?

- Can my child do the app alone?

- Can my child use it and will they like it?

- What grade level is best for this particular app?

- Is the app free or is there a one-time fee or a monthly fee? The right to accommodations, which includes assistive technology, is free of charge to you if your child has a 504 plan.

Always check reviews of any app you buy or use and try it before you give it to your child. The most thorough professionals who evaluate apps for children with learning differences are found at Understood.org, Common Sense Media, and www.dyslexia.com. These companies have a current list of the best apps for children and comprehensive reviews of many of them.

Make sure the therapist you choose is knowledgeable about educational apps and uses them in addition to their lessons with your child. The child must feel successful for the app to be a good teaching tool. To find the right apps that will help your child with a specific subject area, ask your child's teacher, the tech teacher at your school, or the educational specialist chosen to work with your child.

ASSISTIVE TECHNOLOGY

Assistive technology (AT) refers to any item, piece of equipment, device, or software program that can help children with learning differences. AT can aid them in school to become more successful in a variety of subjects, and this, in turn, builds confidence. AT can even be clay, marker boards, yellow markers for highlighting important information, hearing aids, or *anything* that enables children with learning differences to accomplish tasks. AT helps students function in class and hopefully helps them to become more independent. I've seen it work, but children with speech, language, or hearing differences may still have difficulties. For example, my students with speech differences cannot use speech-to-text technology, which lets you talk into the computer and have the computer type out what you said. If they're saying sounds incorrectly, the words will not come out spelled correctly on the screen.

Assistive Technology for Reading

Here is a list of specific technologies for you to consider for your child:

Text to speech (TTS) apps and programs allow your child to see the text and hear it read at the same time.

Audiobooks and digital TTS, like the app Audible, provide books that are read aloud that your child can listen to.

The cost is either monthly or on a per book basis. My students love this. We live in Los Angeles, so they are often stuck in long car rides. I find listening to audiobooks increases their love of reading, motivates them to learn to read, increases their knowledge of vocabulary, and develops their ability to write better because they hear how stories work, with character development, problems, and conclusions. Your child is probably reading books way below their interest level if they have difficulties reading. With Audible they can hear good literature and nonfiction read to them. My students enjoy Bookshare.org, which has a membership for people with disabilities and is provided free to students, Voice Dream Reader for text to speech, and Learningally.org audio books. There are many options to choose from. Professionals from your school or your child's therapist can help you with the latest apps that might work for your child.

Dictionary and thesaurus apps allow children to look up words by voice or image.

Highlighting and annotation tools allow your child to take notes on the content they are reading on screen.

Display controls adjust the font, size, and spacing of the textual content on screen.

Screen masking hides portions of the screen, allowing for fewer distractions, making it easier to focus on the content at hand.

Graphic organizers allow your child to visually outline the content they have read in order to gain a better understanding of it.

Assistive Technology for Writing

Dictation types out what a child says without having to know how the words are spelled. However, if your child has a speech difference, the computer may fail at converting their words to text.

Word prediction helps predict what a child is trying to say and helps finish incomplete thoughts.

Spell check and grammar check help children fix errors in their writing.

Dictionaries and thesauri allow children to look up words by voice or image.

Graphic organizers allow your child to visually outline the content they are trying to write and have it better organized before putting it to paper.

As an educator, I have found I can work with students with different apps, but the minute they start working with a parent, the same child becomes upset. Unless you have a child who works really well with you, it's best to leave the teaching to the professionals. What you can do with your child on the computer is involve them with news. Every student I've worked with loves interesting news articles. Whether it's the story about the dead whale who washed up on shore with 48 pounds of plastic inside him, resulting in the government banning plastic plates and straws, or the man who won over $1.8 million on the show *Jeopardy*, interesting articles make great conversations. You read about the plastic, and the next day in the car you can talk about your child's opinion of the article or have them retell their favorite facts from it. Put their facts or opinions about articles on a board in their room or the family room.

Below is a list of websites for news for your child:

- *The Week Junior*

- Newsela

- *Time for Kids*

- *Washington Post* KidsPost

- *New York Times* Kids section

- DOGOnews

- Common Sense Media lists many more sites that your child may enjoy.

In all my years of teaching, this story is the most unbelievable. But it happened to be one of the best days of my life.

Alex loved Google and so did I. We always went to Google to answer our questions or find interesting facts. One day, Alex asked me what I did before Google. I laughed. "I went to a place called a library and looked up facts in something called a book."

Soon after this conversation, I went to Argentina and met a family with two kids. The family was from Mountain View, California. A bell went off in my head. Google headquarters. It turned out the dad was an executive at Google. By the time we left

Argentina, Ralph said I could bring Alex on a field trip to the Google campus.

When I got home, Alex and I did massive research on the internet about everything having to do with Google, from how it started to how it grew. By the time our field trip came, he had the most incredible questions prepared for Ralph:

What was the most interesting project you worked on at Google?

Did you ever see the first Google computer at Stanford that was made of LEGO bricks?

You have 25 restaurants here. Which is your favorite?

What is your favorite perk from working here?

If I work here, can I take my hamster to work? (Dogs are allowed.)

Alex used technology and all of his executive functions to learn all about Google! The big day came. We had a tour of Google. Alex was quite impressed with the fact that in every single room there is a huge bowl of every kind of candy you could dream of, and it was all free and you could take as much as you wanted. I was most impressed that if you brought your laundry in the morning, they had it finished by the time you went home. But, most important, you could bring your dog to work. Alex has stayed in touch with Ralph, our Google executive friend, for five years. And of course I hope Alex will work at Google one day!

THE TAKEAWAY

There are as many ways for kids to use technology as there are kids! Working with your child and the team you've assembled, you'll be able to figure out which devices and other resources work best with your child's unique learning style and differences.

More broadly, schools need to change the way students learn. Instead of teaching to memorize information, teach other methods on how to obtain the information when they need it. The latest research concludes that tests do not necessarily predict how smart or successful a student with learning differences can be. They can learn new information by accessing it through other methods like technology.

[17]

You know, it's much easier reading to you.

Something to Bark About

K9 Reading Buddies of the North Shore of Chicago has a program where children read to dogs, part of the journey to literacy. Their belief is that "by building a positive association around reading, you'll encourage your child to take it up as a hobby. Regular reading improves their imagination, memory, and more, so you'll give them a useful hobby that will benefit them throughout their life."

———————— // ————————

"I love reading to my dog because he doesn't make me sound out the words," one of my first graders told me when I introduced him to Project R.E.A.D. (Read Everything to a Dog), a program I started when I was a reading teacher in Los Angeles in 1993.

I love dogs. In fact, I love all animals and animal stories, but dogs are my favorite. In the '90s I had a dog named Kugel, named after a Jewish dish with noodles. She was especially responsive to children. I taught her to dance the macarena when she heard that song. Her dance was a bit different from the one kids were doing. She put up one paw, then the other, lay down, rolled over, got up, and barked. She talked all the time. I'm not sure what she was saying, but she talked to every child she ever met.

MY FOUR-LEGGED ASSISTANT TEACHER

The relationship between a child and a pet is one of the most powerful in the world, especially for a child who is having difficulties in school. I began using dogs to help children feel good while they were learning to read after I saw the emotional reaction of the students with my dog, Kugel.

In my pull-out reading program in LA where I helped children learn to read and write, I taught seven students at a time for half an hour in a tiny room with a slanted roof. The room was behind the stage at the school and was used as a dressing room when plays were put on. There was only one small window in the room, situated on the very bottom of the slanted ceiling. Hundreds of books that I collected over many years were on the floor-to-ceiling shelves, and two small tables had been pushed together to seat me and my seven students.

The R.E.A.D. program started because whenever I talked about my Labrador retriever, Kugel, the kids wanted to meet her. And all but one of my students owned dogs. The one who didn't had a grandmother who lived next door with a dog. So, she read to her grandmother's dog.

One homework assignment that's very common in the early grades is to have your child read for 20 minutes a night. But my nonreaders did not want to read for 20 minutes—not to mention the parent's dilemma of having to decide which books to have them read. Instead of having them say, "Here's a book, read for 20 minutes," I wondered what would happen if they were saying, "Honey, read to Rover today. I think he needs a good dog book." Much more motivating.

LET'S READ TO ROVER

And that's when the idea for R.E.A.D. hit. I turned my small room into a "Dog Room," gathered every easy dog book I could find, and placed them all over the room. Children scrambled to take a dog book home each night and practiced reading to their dogs. The results were astonishing. Parents were amazed. Their children came home and "wanted to read" to the dog. Children who had never picked up a book begged their parents to get dog books. They *read* every night. No whining, no crying.

Then everyone wrote about their dogs. Pictures of their dogs were tacked on the slanted ceiling. They also wanted to research their dogs. We looked up facts about dogs (there was no Google back then) and created "how to act" rules for when a dog came into the room.

Here are the dog, kid, and owner rules made up by my students:

> Rules for dogs:
>
> - No pooping on the carpet or peeing in the corners.
>
> - Practice your tricks before you come to class so you can do them here.
>
> - The toys in Dr. Waller's room cannot be chewed.
>
> - Do not chew on the books.
>
> - Focus on the story being read to you.
>
> - Be a good listener.
>
> - Be nice to all the kids.
>
> - Don't bark and scare the kids.
>
> - Do not eat from the trash can.
>
> - Only lick kids who want to be licked.

And truthfully, I don't know why but no dogs were bad dogs. I just think the dogs "knew" it was important that they behave. And don't forget the children were reading to their dogs every night at home.

> Rules for kids:
>
> - Ask the dog's owner if you can pet the dog.
>
> - One person at a time can pet the dog.

- One person at a time can read to the dog.

- Ask the owner if the dog can do any tricks.

- Don't say anything if the dog is ugly because it will hurt the owner's feelings, and probably the dog's, too.

Rules for owners:

- Make sure your dog likes kids.

- Make sure your dog has pooped and peed before you come to the class.

- Bring dog treats to school.

- Keep the dog on a leash.

- Say "sit" to your dog.

- Introduce the dog to everyone.

- Tell us your dog's name.

- Make sure to tell the kids if the dog licks because some kids don't like to be licked.

- Tell us how you got your dog.

- Tell us a story about your dog.

Each child brought their dog to school and they read to it. Then the other children got to read to the dog, too. After each dog left my reading center, the children wrote about the dog visit. All the stories and dog facts and the "Dog Rules" lists were put into a book.

For the final activity, we invited all the parents and dogs to a Bark Mitzvah, where the students served dog bones to the dogs and dog bones made out of peanut butter, dry milk, honey, and graham crackers to the parents. Each child got up on the stage and read a poem they had written about their dog to the entire group of adults and kids—over 80 people.

What was the magic? Children who hated reading were becoming readers. They became confident and were *happy*! Children knew if they made a mistake, the dog wouldn't correct them or make them sound out words. And the child wouldn't see the frustrated face of a teacher or parent when they didn't know a word.

Many years later my student Alex, who loved to cook and owned a hamster, wrote many books about the friendship of his hamster, Gerald, and my new dog, Carat. He even staged the photographs he took for books he wrote using Carat and Gerald, who loved each other.

EVERYTHING'S BETTER WITH DOGS

There are now studies proving what I concluded in 1993: children become more fluent in reading when reading to dogs and they are calmer when dogs are present. The University of California, Davis, Veterinary Medicine Extension did a study in 2010 and concluded that in 10 weeks elementary students improved their fluency in reading by 12% and home-schooled children increased their fluency by 30% by reading to a dog. And the children felt more confident in their reading skills.

The Sit Stay Read Program in 2009 at National Louis University also measured reading fluency in children who read to a dog; those children increased their reading fluency by 20% compared to the control group, who did not read to a dog.

Check your local library for dog reading days. Many libraries around the country do it now after seeing how successful it can be with promoting reading. Or organize a dog reading day with other parents and children with dogs or pets. It can be a wonderful experience for your child to help in the planning, invitations, rules, food . . . talk about executive functioning! A dog day can help your child with many skills and really help their self-confidence.

No matter what pet you own—dog, cat, hamster, mouse, snake, fish, or any other—you can use the strong relationship your child has with the pet to get your child reading and writing. Remember, usually pets like stories about their species. Dogs do not like cat books! Hamsters are not very focused! Here are some ideas:

- Make up a story using the pet as the main character. Your child can dictate the story to you if they want to, and you can type it for them. Keep all stories in a three-ring binder. Kids love to go back and reread or have the story read to them.

- Take pictures of the pet to add to the story book.

- Have your child plan a birthday for their pet. Brainstorm what food will be needed and whom to invite. Make sure your child is very involved with the planning. This will help with executive functioning. Make sure to tell the children if the dog licks because some children don't like to be licked.

- Research interesting facts about your pet on Google and find books that relate to your animal. This will help them with researching skills.

- Find easy books that your child can read to their pet. You can read the book first aloud, and then ask your child to read it to their pet.

One day, seven-year-old Maya came running into class yelling, "Dr. Waller, Mom said I can have a dog when I'm 15." She was so excited, and I'm sure not so good at math, but I hoped she'd get a fish, hamster, gerbil, or *something* before 15. Many years later, I ran into the mom and asked if Maya ever got her dog. "Yes," she replied, "when she was 15. But I didn't realize in three years she'd be leaving for college and leaving me to care for *her* dog."

THE TAKEAWAY

If your child has learning differences, consider getting a pet early on. Children can gain confidence and companionship from the relationship they have with their pet, and you can do a number of fun activities with reading to and writing about their pet. If your child does not have a real pet, have them read to their "stuffie" (stuffed animal). Believe me, stuffies won't criticize your child's reading either!

[18]

Avoiding Meltdowns
During School Breaks

Charles Schwab, founder and chairman of the Charles
Schwab Corporation, who has lived with learning differences, once stated that "to sit down with a blank piece
of paper and write was the most traumatic thing that ever
faced me in life." Some bumps in the road will always happen, but here are some strategies for avoiding distress.

———————————— // ————————————

Ryan is one of the many students with learning differences who
can't wait for vacation breaks. During the school year, everyone looks forward to a school break. "Not you, Vicki," Ryan,

a first-grade student with learning differences, said before he headed off to holiday on winter break. "You just love to teach kids every day, make them practice reading books, writing stories, and paying attention. You don't care about vacations."

"Are you kidding?" I asked him. "Do you think I love to get up at 7 a.m., go on school visits, talk to your speech therapist, occupational therapist, and teachers; teach you using your passion for Roblox; stay up late writing what we did in our session; and talk to your parents? Really, really? My brain gets full just like yours. All I want to do is go on vacation and do whatever I want. I love to sleep in, travel all over to see interesting countries filled with wonderful animals, and eat pizza and candy every day."

WORKING WITH WONDERFUL CHAOS

A few weeks before school ends for winter, spring, or summer break, classrooms are usually on a different schedule. The class may be preparing for a party or an open house or practicing for a parent performance. Students are cleaning their desks and finishing projects. This is wonderful chaos for the child who has learning differences because there is a smaller amount of work and a lot less strain on the brain!

Home may be different, too. Homework is lighter, and there's less stress and arguing about homework. Sleep times may be looser. The family might be excited, planning for vacation. The child is faced with fewer expectations.

Still, children with attention issues, even on medicine, can also be difficult during this time because the structure at school and home is less strict. Children might enjoy less homework, but they still need structure, and they may actually feel anxiety as their parents get ready to go away.

Before leaving on a trip:

- Try to keep your child's sleep schedule the same. If not, your child may get tired, and that's when meltdowns can start.

- If your child seems nervous or is a worrier, you can have a family meeting to discuss your upcoming trip. Talk about: transport to your destination, what they can take on the plane or in the car, seating arrangements, what you'll do if the plane is delayed, where you're staying and for how long, sleeping arrangements, and sites you may see.

- Go online to look at your destination. Show your child the sites; ask what they might like to do.

- Give your child a list of what to take. Lay out underwear, shorts, bathing suits, cover-ups, a hat, books, and a favorite game. Make sure they take some word games, playing cards, crossword puzzles, activity books, and maze books. If you foresee they will be on their tablets, National Geographic's *Weird but True!* app can be a good one.

- Make a chart on a piece of paper with days of the week on it a week before you leave on your trip. On each day's square write a suggestion of what they can do that night for their upcoming trip. For example, on Monday decide which toy or stuffie they want to take with them, on Tuesday which game they want to take, etc. Each night they pack the items on the chart, then cross it off on the chart.

Teachers might think it's a good idea to give the students reading or activities to do on their vacations. And parents, striving to get their child to where they should be academically, may want to use this time to push academics. But children with learning differences are freaked by these assignments when they are on vacation. So, don't tell them about all the reading and writing you want them to do on the trip. Instead, make the learning fun.

More trip suggestions:

- Go online and look for books together. Joke books, poetry books, *National Geographic* magazines, and *The Week Junior* are great for vacations. Your child can also choose a chapter book you can read to them on the trip.

- Put some audible books on their tablet. They can listen to the books in the car or on the plane. The school librarian or teachers often have helpful suggestions.

- Don't forget a journal so your child can use it to write about the trip or paste postcards from the vacation. You can bring tape or a glue stick to make this easier.

- Before you leave on the trip, check with your child's doctor about medication for your child. Some parents take their kids off meds before vacation. But parents who do this often come back and say it was a dreadful trip. The child got into fights with siblings, wasn't focused, and generally was out of control.

Without talking to their doctor, Mitchell and Steve had decided to take Alex off his meds to give him a break on vacation during his second-grade year. Steve called to tell me they made a really poor decision. "He was so unfocused, argued with everyone, fought with all his siblings, and didn't sleep at all. And, of course, he did no reading the entire time, so he came home and cried all night."

Similarly kids off meds going to summer camp have found they are inattentive at playing sports and are more impulsive. Sleepaway camps have medical personnel who can administer medication to your child.

On the trip:

- During vacation, try to see if you can maintain the flow by keeping your child on medication.

- Keep their sleeping and eating schedule steady.

- Try to monitor junk food.

- Be aware of overprogramming.

- Make sure in general that your child is involved in the planning of activities and has a sense of what you are going to do.

- Schedule downtime when you can. If your child wants to stay around the hotel or go to a park, downtime can really help to do that.

- Keep your child engaged and make sure they do their school assignments. Have them write what they did each day in a journal.

> • Find postcards on your trip so they can write a sentence or two about what they did that day. Or they can draw what they did. They won't have to ask "What do I write?" because they had the experience. You may have to help with spelling, but if you do it each night, there will be at least 20 sentences for 10 nights. Not only does your child have the writing assignment finished, but they have a wonderful memory of the trip. This can help with post-vacation meltdown.

Lucy, a second grader, was supposed to write two sentences a night over vacation. Not difficult right? But she carried on so much that her parents gave up asking her to do it. Ten days later, 20 sentences were due at school, and the crying and tantruming really started. I got a hysterical phone call from the mom. I told her to have Lucy write five sentences about what she liked on the trip. "That will be easy," I told her. "Send it with a note to the teacher, asking if she can finish the next night." Of course, the teacher said OK, and it took Lucy a very short time the next night to write about what she'd loved on the trip.

Children can also look at photos you took on the trip on your phone and write a sentence or two. You can put the printed pictures and sentences into a blank book—Ashley Blank Books on Amazon is a good place to get these—or on a piece of paper. Joey, my student who loved soccer, went on a trip and saw a soccer game. He wrote and wrote because he wanted to tell everything about every player. He wrote more than the ten sentences required by his teacher. And no crying!

If your child has reading assignments during vacation, make sure you keep up with them. Sherri, mom of Denise, a third grader, called me at 9 p.m. the night before school was going to begin again after winter break. Apparently, Denise was supposed to read every night on their vacation, but every night there was a screaming argument about it, and the mom couldn't take it, so they had done no schoolwork, including the reading log she was supposed to do. The second they arrived home, Denise got completely overwhelmed.

Try to make sure the assignments get done, and don't wait until the end of vacation. Remember that reading time during vacation doesn't have to be done right before bed; you can always do it while you are waiting for dinner to arrive or at the beach.

THE TAKEAWAY

The best way to avoid stress and meltdowns is to be prepared for the vacation. For children and adults, it takes time to get adjusted when you get back home. Let your kids know your feelings, too. A vacation should be stress-free, and using some of the ideas in this chapter will help that to happen.

[19]

How to Avoid Back-to-School Hysteria

Whoopi Goldberg, actress and talk show host, had a mother who told her she wasn't stupid and could grow up to be and do anything she wanted. Whoopi always thought, "I [knew I] couldn't be stupid because if you read to me, I would tell you everything you read." If every child had this self-confidence, school would be a lot less fraught for many.

———————— // ————————

Summer is a great time for any child, especially for those with learning differences. There's less anxiety and stress in the summer. No school means no homework, fewer tablet rules, staying up later than usual, and fun times with the family. Even if your child still goes to therapists in the summer, no school means the load is lighter.

For you, the morning may be less rushed because you are not packing lunches or worrying about your child forgetting their homework and their backpack. There are no afternoon conferences or emails asking you to come in, and you may have a more relaxed atmosphere in your home: family trips, relatives visiting from out of town, and adventures. If you are a working parent, you have probably already planned summer activities and have babysitters lined up to take your child to their therapists' appointments.

So what's the key to avoiding that inevitable back-to-school hysteria?

BE READY FOR BACK-TO-SCHOOL STRESS

Two weeks before the school year begins, everyone is back home and hysterical that school is starting. The closer to school beginning, the worse the anxiety. You may be starting to worry about your child already. Who is the teacher? Will they understand your child? Will your child be able to learn this year? Will your child be in a class with some friends, and not the bully from last year?

Take a deep breath. These inner feelings may not go away, but if you make a family plan and use these two weeks to prepare, it can help both your child's anxiety and your own.

The family plan before school begins in fall:

- First, make sure conversations about your concerns for your child take place away from the child. It's common to think children aren't listening. Believe me, even at three years old, your child will know when you are talking anxiously about them!

- If for some reason you took your child off medication for the summer but plan to have them take meds in school, now is the time to see the doctor so your child can adjust to the meds before school starts. If possible, three weeks before school is best.

- Most children go to bed later in the summer because the sun is out longer and everything goes easier at bedtime. About two weeks before school starts, begin putting your child to sleep about 15 minutes earlier than the summer schedule.

- Maybe you didn't read to your child each night during the summer. Begin reading a chapter book or funny poetry each night.

- Before bed, ask what makes them happy, what they are worried about, and how you can help. Talk about all the things your child is good at. Remind them what they *do* like about school. You are slowly getting them ready to get back into

> school. Then, two weeks later when school starts, they will have transitioned back to "school time."
>
> - At one point during these two weeks, talk to your child about what interesting and fun activities your family did this summer. Take pictures from your phone, print them out, and paste them in a blank book or staple pieces of paper together like a book. Have your child write a sentence about each picture. Younger children can dictate the words to you and you can type the words and paste them into the book under the pictures. You'll be surprised how the young child will "read" it back to you. Do this because the first day of school, the teacher often asks the class to write about summer vacation, and this can be the start of stress for your child.

Jennifer, going into fourth grade, was a wreck before school began. When we talked about it, she said she felt dumb, had trouble writing stories, and was worried the new teacher would be mean to her because she had learning differences. Jennifer had gone to sleepaway camp that summer, and I asked her to tell me five activities she did at camp that she loved. She easily told me 10. By the time we were finished, I wished I had gone with her. I had her write simple sentences about each activity and why she liked it. We worked on a topic sentence and an ending sentence. She looked at her finished sentences and was so surprised she had written them.

When her teacher asked the class to write what they did over the summer, Jennifer was prepared.

"How did you know, Vicki?" Jennifer asked when I saw her that week for therapy.

I laughed. "All teachers give that assignment in the first week in every elementary grade classroom in the world!"

More thoughts for before school starts:

- During the daytime in the car, before school begins, start talking about school. Listen when they say they're scared. Try to be supportive. You can say, "Yes, I know you're scared. And I am here to help you, and you have a wonderful therapist [I hope you do] to work with you on your schoolwork. You will be able to succeed. Some things might be hard, but we are going to get you through them." Remind your child again what they are good at.

- Tell them the teachers are scared, too. Teachers don't know who will be in their classes. They've been on vacation and sleeping in every day and not having to do work or go to meetings. "They feel just as you do!" If you're going back to work, tell them how you feel.

- Ask them what they are looking forward to. In my experience, when students are asked what they like best about school, the answer is often recess. But after some prodding, they might say art or science or library, or when the teacher reads to them.

- Talk about their fall weekly schedule, including when they play sports, when they will see their therapist, and when they have music lessons and so on.

- Remind them of the rules for the tablet or other devices, too, so they are not shocked that after school with activities and homework there might be less time for electronics (if that is your rule).

- You can check the class list and see who is in their class to invite over. Then arrange playdates with children they may not have seen all summer so they will be prepared socially.

- The weekend before school, try to do a family outing. Maybe go to a movie.

- Once school starts, you want at least one parent there during bedtime to talk about that first week of school and how it is going for them.

THE TAKEAWAY

Notice I didn't say anything about talking to the teacher about your child. At the beginning of the year, the teacher has no idea who your child is, and they are so busy with everything that it isn't usually a good time to talk. You can email them, introducing yourself and your child who has learning differences, but the real talk should be after a few weeks, when you can ask if you might set up a meeting with the teacher and your child's therapist or specialist.

These suggestions for before school starts are here to help ease the anxiety for you *and* your child. All this won't happen right away, but if you plan a few weeks before school starts, a day at a time, then hopefully there will be less stress for your child and . . . *you!*

[20]

A Word of Hope

Former Vermont governor Peter Shumlin, who has learning differences, spoke to students with learning differences at Eagle High School's commencement ceremony. He told them, "Embrace your nontraditional learning style as a gift."

———————————— // ————————————

In April 2015, I attended a Friends of the Semel Institute for Neuroscience and Human Behavior fundraiser at UCLA. The Friends of the Semel Institute is a volunteer organization dedicated to supporting and enhancing state-of-the-art research and treatment for illnesses of the mind and brain. One of the speakers was Susan Lerner, a board member of this organization, who was speaking on children with learning differences and ADHD. She started out by telling the audience she was the mother of four ADHD adult children, and eight of her 12 grandchildren had ADHD and other learning, processing, or anxiety differences.

Because of his hyperactivity and processing challenges, her oldest son had always had a tough time in school. Partway through one of his school years, she learned that his desk had been placed outside the hallway as punishment. He had to look inside the open door of the classroom to participate. In 10th grade, his math teacher said to Susan, "I'm sorry, your son has no ability to go to college. You must be realistic."

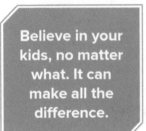

Believe in your kids, no matter what. It can make all the difference.

Her son would eventually receive his MBA from the Marshall School at USC. And when he did, he thanked his mother for believing in him.

Over 30 years ago, when Susan's twins were in seventh grade, a wonderful teacher in London, where they had moved for a few years, suggested she get her twin girls tested for severe learning differences. Their grades were good, but they were unable to organize properly. "You have two mediocre girls," the psychologist who did the testing said to Susan. "They will never be able to read great books, but they might be able to read Agatha Christie. They probably won't be able to read the *London Times*, but they may be able to read those inferior celebrity newspapers."

The psychologist, not knowing much about learning differences, suggested Susan put the twins in group therapy. Susan's daughters were the only two students in the group who had not been in jail. Finally, with Susan's tenacity, the twins got the help they needed. Now one is a lawyer and the other is an endocrinologist.

Because Susan's children had learning differences and ADHD, when they had kids of their own they were aware of the issues their children had and how to help them early on so they weren't stigmatized.

One grandson has both learning differences and physical challenges. He underwent many therapies his whole life, including therapy for low motor tone, which affected his talking and his walking. Now he is an excellent water polo player and got accepted to both MIT and Harvard. Susan concluded, "Just think—we had been afraid he wouldn't walk."

What I loved about this story was that the whole multi-generational family was involved. Grandparents play a very important part in their children's lives when they believe in their grandchildren and never give up. Connecting a child to grandparents is probably the most wonderful relationship in the world.

For four years, 30 years ago, I connected my students to elderly residents in an assisted-living home. I called it the Printer Pal Program. I received a grant to buy a computer for the home and was amazed to find that the residents could actually type on the computer because many had used typewriters all their lives. They were ages 84 to 94 and how quickly they learned to use the computer! My students researched what the times were like when these elderly women (there were no men in this facility) lived and typed questions and sent them by email to the home.

The students asked about presidents alive at their time, favorite hobbies, and vacations. Many memories included life during the Depression, five-cent movies, berry picking, hayrides, killing and cleaning chickens in their backyards, and keeping live fish in their bathtubs to make a fish meal for dinner.

The residents received the letters, and once a week my teenage son and I went to the home and helped the residents type letters, answering the questions my students asked. The students then met their "printer pals" once a year at a luncheon at our school. My students became very involved with their printer pals and loved meeting them at the end of the year. For the elderly it was a stroll down memory lane. They loved remembering, and they felt worthwhile.

Because I saw the importance of the elderly in the lives of children and vice versa, I encouraged and taught my students to do oral histories of their own grandparents. Then I videoed them interviewing their grandparents. I was awarded the *Los Angeles Times* Local Hero Award for my Printer Pal Program, helping to bridge the generations. And I hope, more than anything, my students found a new interest in their grandparents and what their lives were like.

One of the best letters I received was from a former student's mother:

"My son learned to read from you many years ago. When he was nine, you did a project with him where he made up questions for his grandfather and then did an oral history of him. His grandpa, my dad, passed away recently. While cleaning out his apartment, I found the video marked, 'Mikey and grandpa, never tape over.'

"Mikey and I watched it yesterday, just a day after his 29th birthday. I'm sure we watched it many years ago, but I really didn't remember it. It was so wonderful to see my dad again and learn stuff that I never knew, or had forgotten. So really, I can't thank you enough for teaching my son to read and doing such a meaningful project with him. A gift to our family!"

As parents (or educators wanting to do a fabulous project), you can have your child (or students) do an oral history of their grandparents by writing questions, interviewing them, and filming the project. It makes a memory to keep forever and a bond that lasts a lifetime.

THE TAKEAWAY

There is constant research being done on learning differences. Parents, grandparents, teachers, researchers, and educators are becoming more aware now than ever before. With the right support, every child can succeed just like the students I teach and continue to fight for. We have it within our power to help more and more children focus on their strengths, not their weaknesses, and their abilities not their disabilities. And most important, we can help children use their amazing passions to live happy lives, doing what they love.

[21]

> Don't give up on yourself or your
> dreams.
> You're worthwhile, and always will be,
> no matter what.
> Just remember to always be who you
> are, because that person is very special.
> There's no person in the whole world
> like you.
> And I like you just the way you are.
>
> Mr. Fred Rogers

A Perfect Final Ending to This Book from Alex the Chef

I asked Alex, now 16 years old, to write a blurb for the book. He said he was so lucky that he had me as an educational therapist who not only knew how to teach him with his learning differences but made him realize he was smart. He said he was grateful I used all his strengths and passions to teach him and make reading fun.

———————— // ————————

This book started because I worked with my elementary student Alex from the end of first grade through fourth grade.

As a student with learning differences and ADHD/Inattentive, he attended a school that required all professionals working with their students to write weekly updates on the child's progress.

Alex is now in high school, 16 years old and 5 feet 10 inches. He is still on medication for his attention and has an educational therapist to assist him in organizing and studying for his seven classes. He is also a great reader and writer who does well in school and is interested in many subjects.

I was invited to Alex's Bar Mitzvah, the Jewish rite of passage for a 13-year-old boy to become a man. Alex had asked me to be part of his service and gave me the honor of opening the arc where the Torah was located. The room was filled with his friends and family. He stood there, looking confident, not scared at all, in front of 200 people. Toward the end of the service, after he'd read Hebrew from the Torah, he gave a speech in which he related his own life to the story of Noah and the Arc. Alex told how the world had gotten to a very bad place when God told Noah to build an arc and bring on two of every nonkosher animal and seven of every kosher animal. It took Noah 120 years to build the arc, and once the flood began, his family and the animals lived on the arc for 365 days.

Alex explained the suffering Noah endured. The days were filled with very hard work and horrific conditions. He never gave up, and he was rewarded with a promise that God would never eradicate humanity again.

This story, Alex explained to us, is about the power of patience and how without it anything that is challenging will never get accomplished. Patience is a test to see how passionate we are about the goal we are pursuing. "It's easy to give up after you've fallen down," Alex said. "But you pull yourself up and continue to try, even though you know you may fall down a lot! That's when we gain our power, when we persevere."

Alex related this story to his homework, how time consuming and stressful it could be. "But if you can take a deep breath and plan for yourself, you will be able to persevere." He explained that sometimes that means asking for help when you need it, even if you are afraid of what other people will think. And having faith in yourself. "Faith is just a fancy way of saying 'trust,'" Alex said. "When you trust, you are depending on someone or something outside of yourself."

He acknowledged how hard it is to have patience, especially when doing something for the first time. "You prepare the cake, and the cake goes in, and you know not to open the oven, but you want to open it. You know the right amount of time has not passed, but that is where patience comes in," Alex said.

He concluded by giving the lesson he hoped everyone would gain from his speech. "Remember that patience, faith, and perseverance will help you tremendously. Noah probably felt very accomplished from all of his hard work. If any of you have goals in your life, whether they are big or small, just remember to keep going." Very wise words from a very wise student with learning differences who perseveres and keeps going!

And in answer to his question how old I'll be when he goes to college and if I can go with him . . . hopefully he won't need me!

My Favorite Books for Children Pre-K Through Grade 6

There are many genres of books. I have chosen just a few and divided my list into books that have been popular with my students for years.

———————— // ————————

- Early readers board books (0–3 years)
- Books for ages 3–7
- Fiction
- Graphic novels
- Nonfiction
- Poetry

Early Readers Board Books, 0–3 Years

Board books are my favorites because they are hard to rip or chew. These are short books with bright colors and usually feature words that repeat or rhyme. There are literally hundreds to choose from, but, truthfully, you can't go wrong with any. You can start reading these books when your baby is born.

> Boynton, Sandra
> > *Big Box of Boynton* books
> > *The Going to Bed Book*
> > *Snuggle Puppy*
> Dorling Kindersley board books
> > *Baby Faces*
> > the various *Peekaboo!* books
> McBratney, Sam and Anita Jeram
> > *Guess How Much I Love You?*
> Priddy, Roger
> > *First 100 Words*
> > *Bright Baby Colors, ABC, Numbers*

Wordless Picture Books, 3–7 Years

These are books with pictures but no words, so your child can make up the story as they see the pictures. I love picture books with great stories and illustrations. I think the best wordless picture books are by Mercer Mayer about a boy, a dog, and a frog.

> Day, Alexandra
> > All her Carl the dog books
> Mayer, Mercer
> > All his *Boy, Dog, and Frog* books

Books with Great Stories and Pictures, 3–7 Years

These books can start out as "read alouds" with your child. The stories are classics and never get old being read aloud or being read by your child as they become readers.

Arnold, Tedd
> The *Fly Guy* series is hilarious.

Barraca, Debra and Sal
> *The Adventures of Taxi Dog*

Bridwell, Norman
> *Clifford the Big Red Dog*

Buehner, Caralyn and Mark Buehner
> *Snowmen*
> *The Escape of Marvin the Ape*

Carle, Eric
> *The Very Hungry Caterpillar* (A great book to read; and then order a Butterfly Garden Kit from Insect Lore. You are sent five live caterpillars and your child watches over two weeks as they turn into butterflies.)

dePaola, Tomie
> *Strega Nona*

Eastman, P. D.
> *Are You My Mother?*

Feiffer, Jules
> *Bark, George!*

Garcia, Gabi
> *I Can Do Hard Things: Mindful Affirmations for Kids*

Henkes, Kevin
> Every story book he has written. His books for older kids are also incredible.

Kotzwinkle, William
> *Walter the Farting Dog*

Laden, Nina
    The Night I Followed the Dog
    When Pigasso Met Mootisse
    Peek-a Who? Boxed Set
Lobel, Arnold
    The *Frog and Toad* series
Meyers, Susan
    Everywhere Babies
Munsch, Robert
    All his books are hilarious.
Novak, B. J.
    The Book with No Pictures
Numeroff, Laura
    If You Give the Mouse a Cookie
Rinker, Sherri Duskey
    Good Night, Good Night Construction Site
Saltzberg, Barney
    All his books for little ones and older ones
    are fantastic.
Seuss, Dr. Theodor (Theodor Seuss Geisel)
    Green Eggs and Ham
Steig, William
    The Amazing Bone
    Amos & Boris
    Sylvester and the Magic Pebble
Tamaki, Jillian
    They Say Blue
Van Allsburg, Chris
    The Mysteries of Harris Burdick

Viorst, Judith
  Alexander and the Terrible, Horrible, No Good,
  Very Bad Day
Waber, Bernard
  Lyle, Lyle, Crocodile
Willems, Mo
  Don't Let the Pigeon Drive the Bus!
  Knuffle Bunny
Williams, Vera
  More More More Said the Baby

Chapter Books for Ages 7–12

These are my favorite chapter books for children in elementary school. Some can be read aloud earlier, some are for children who already read. Always check with your school librarian or child's teacher if the topic of the story is age-appropriate for your child, and of course check if the story is one your child would be interested in.

Alifirenka, Caitlin and Martin Ganda
  I Will Always Write Back
Applegate, Katherine
  The One and Only Ivan, but actually all her books
  are terrific.
Babbitt, Natalie
  Tuck Everlasting
Bellairs, John
  The Treasure of Alpheus Winterborn
Blume, Judy
  Tales of a Fourth Grade Nothing

Bunting, Eve
  Sixth-Grade Sleepover (This book is about a sleepover I had with my students!)
Cleary, Beverly
  Dear Mr. Henshaw
Clements, Andrew
  Frindle
  The Report Card
Curtis, Christopher Paul
  The Watsons Go to Birmingham 1963
Dahl, Roald
  Charlie and the Chocolate Factory
  James and the Giant Peach
DiCamillo, Kate
  Because of Winn-Dixie
  The Tale of Despereaux
Gantos, Jack
  The *Joey Pigza* series
Gardiner, John Reynolds
  Stone Fox
Gannett, Ruth Stiles
  My Father's Dragon
Glaser, Karina Yan
  The Vanderbeekers of 141st Street
Griffin, Paul
  When Friendship Followed Me Home
Henkes, Kevin
  The Year of Billy Miller and his many other books, all great.
Howe, Deborah and James
  Bunnicula

Juster, Norton
The Phantom Tollbooth
Konigsburg, E. L.
From the Mixed-Up Files of Mrs. Basil E. Frankweiler
Lamothe, Matt
This Is How We Do It: One Day in the Lives of Seven Kids from around the World
Levine, Kristin
The Lions of Little Rock
O'Brien, Robert
Mrs. Frisby and the Rats of NIMH
O'Dell, Scott
Island of the Blue Dolphins
Osborne, Mary Pope
The *Magic Tree House* series (great for new readers)
Palacio, R. J.
Wonder
Paterson, Katherine
Bridge to Terabithia
The Great Gilly Hopkins
Paulsen, Gary
Hatchet
Sachar, Louis
Holes
Sideways Stories from Wayside School
Selden, George
The Cricket in Times Square
Spinelli, Jerry
Maniac Magee
Tarshis, Lauren
The *I Survived* series

Thaler, Mike
  Black Lagoon Adventures, a set of small chapter
  books students love!
White, E. B.
  The Trumpet of the Swan
Winkler, Henry
  The *Hank Zipzer* series
Wolk, Lauren
  Beyond the Bright Sea

Graphic Novels for Ages 6–9

If you find your child is reading—or wants *you* to read—a
bunch of these a week and you're worried there are too many
pictures, I am here to tell you, it's *reading*! And your child, if
they are obsessed with books, will continue to stay obsessed
with books and they will begin reading nongraphic novels.
These books are great motivators for reluctant readers or
any child!

Brosgol, Vera
  Be Prepared
Clanton, Ben
  The Narwhal and Jelly series
Craft, Jerry
  New Kid
Blabey, Aaron
  The *Bad Guys* series
Hale, Shannon
  Rapunzel's Revenge
Jun, Nie
  My Beijing: Four Stories of Everyday Wonder

Kinney, Jeff
Diary of a Wimpy Kid series
Martin, Ann M.
The Baby-Sitters Club series
Peirce, Lincoln
The Big Nate series
Pilkey, Dav
The *Captain Underpants* series
The *Dog Man* series
Riordan, Rick
The *Percy Jackson and the Olympians* series
Simpson, Dana
The *Phoebe and Her Unicorn* series
Telgemeier, Raina
Sisters

Nonfiction

Children love nonfiction, especially if it is on topics they are interested in. My favorite publishers are National Geographic and the Dorling Kindersley *Eyewitness* books. The big colorful books on any subject you can think of are breathtaking and entice any child immediately. I also use the *Weird but True!* series all of the time. It has so many fascinating facts!

National Geographic has nonfiction books about famous people that are graded for reading levels. They also have the *Photo Ark* books by Joel Sartore with pictures of amazing animals from all over the world. The *National Geographic Animal Encyclopedia, 125 True Stories of Amazing Animals,* and *5,000 Awesome Facts* are three of my favorites. Their subscription magazine called *Kids* is a winner, too.

The Dorling Kindersley *Eyewitness* books start at baby level and go up to adult. Every subject is touched upon in fabulous books with facts and pictures: sports, space, science, animals, people, first ladies, planets, and insects.

The Week magazine now has a weekly magazine for kids, *The Week Junior*. Every household with kids must have this magazine!

Poetry

I like to read poetry with children and have them make up their own poems. Using these books as a starter list is a fun way to begin.

Harris, Chris
I'm Just No Good at Rhyming
Hughes, Langston
Poetry for Young People
Lansky, Bruce
A Bad Case of the Giggles
If Kids Ruled the School
Miles of Smiles
No More Homework! No More Tests!
Prelutsky, Jack
For Laughing Out Loud
A Pizza the Size of the Sun
Silverstein, Shel
A Light in the Attic
Where the Sidewalk Ends

There are millions of books and many new ones come out each year. Joke books are a favorite of my students, especially at Halloween. Many children like folklore, fantasy, realistic fiction, historical fiction, and biographies. The most important point is to take your child with you to the library or bookstore and spend time there. I can assure you I have never met a child, even a nonreader, who doesn't know what kind of book or story they want to hear or read.

My favorite comprehension questions to ask children during or after reading to them are:

- Can you summarize the story for me?

- What new vocabulary words did you learn?

- Did you learn anything new about the world/ life/this topic/feelings?

- What do you think the characters (or the settings) look like?

- What is the main idea/takeaway/theme of this story?

- Does any of this relate to your own life?

- Tell me the sequence of events.

- What do you think is going to happen next (after the story ends)?

- Compare this book to another book you read.

- Why do you think the author wrote this book?

- What's the biggest problem the main character faces?

- Did you like this book?

- Do you think the author was happy writing this book?

[APPENDIX B]

This is a fun letter game.

High-Frequency Words

The Fry 100 most common words are called high-frequency words because half of every page in every printed material is composed of these 100 words. The first 100 words should be mastered by the end of first grade, the second 100 by the end of second grade, the third 100 by the end of third grade, and the rest of the 1,000 by the end of fifth grade. The words are arranged in order of frequency when they occur in printed material.

———————————————————— // ————————————————————

Many of the words are hard to sound out, or decode, using regular phonics rules. That is why learning the first 100 is very important for the success of early reading.

Here is a list of the 100 high-frequency words:

the	or	will	number
of	one	up	no
and	had	other	way
a	by	about	could
to	words	out	people
in	but	many	my
is	not	then	than
you	what	them	first
that	all	these	water
it	were	so	been
he	we	some	called
was	when	her	who
for	your	would	am
on	can	make	its
are	said	like	now
as	there	him	find
with	use	into	long
his	an	time	down
they	each	has	day
I	which	look	did
at	she	two	get
be	do	more	come
this	how	write	made
have	their	go	may
from	if	see	part

Activities to Help Your Child Learn the 100 High-Frequency Words

As I've talked about in the chapters on reading and writing, making books with your child, even as early as three years old, begins the process of your child seeing that what they say can be written down and actually read.

- If you go on a trip or have a birthday party, take pictures and print them out and ask your child to tell you what the picture is about. Then write the sentence your child says under the picture. Underline the high-frequency words in the sentence. Put the picture with the sentence in your child's room, on the door, in the playroom, or in the kitchen. As you walk by, ask your child to read it. At first, they will remember what they told you to write and so will "read" the sentence. But after a while, they will actually look at the sentence and read it. You can then point to the underlined word and ask them to say it. Believe me, children remember the hard words like Disneyland way before they remember the word "was." But seeing it at a young age over and over in sentences, they'll finally remember when they see it in books.

- Go to this web address to download flash cards for use at home for the Fry 1000 Instant Words:

  www.uniqueteachingresources.com/Fry-1000-Instant-Words.html

YES! YOUR CHILD CAN

- You can print out the flashcards from the site listed above, but I would not do them with small children. And taking the high-frequency words out of a sentence will make it stressful for your child to read or remember. It's better to use the many sentences you write with them to show them these very important 100 words. Then as they get older you can use the flashcards.

- Make a bingo game. Divide three (or more, depending on how many players) 8" x 11" sheets of paper into 25 squares. Choose 25 of the high-frequency words to write in the squares. Do this randomly on each sheet of paper for each player so that all game boards are different. Then print one of the sheets with words and cut the squares out for the words that will be called aloud by the person leading the game. I like putting short sentences in the squares so the child sees the words in the context of a sentence they dictated to you. I use beads as markers. The dealer chooses a word card and calls out the word. When the child finds the word on the bingo sheet, they put a bead on the word. The winner is whoever gets five beads across, down, or diagonally before everyone else does.

- Choose five words from the list. Look in some picture books with your child to find those five words. They are on every page!

- Take sentences from stories your child has dictated to you, write them on paper, and put them up all over the house. Read them as you go by.

- You can use story starters from the internet and say the sentence and ask your child to finish it. Have your child practice using a full sentence to answer the questions. This is fun to do in the car or on a long drive. Later you can write what your child said in a notebook and underline the high-frequency words. Here are some story starters:

  - The thing I'd like someone to know about me is . . . (the, to, me, is)

  - What would you do with $100? I would . . . (what, would, you, do, with, I)

  - What are you good at? I'm good at . . . (what, are, you, at)

  - What is your favorite animal? My favorite animal is . . . because (what, is, your)

  - What is your favorite book and why? My favorite book is . . . because (what, is, your, and)

Play concentration with the words. Take five words and write them on 10 index cards so you end with 10 cards with each word written twice. Turn the cards over so no words are showing. The first player turns over two cards to try to match two words. If they don't match, the player has to turn the two cards over and return them to the exact spot they were in. The next player does the same until two cards match. When two cards match, the player puts them in their pile. They keep doing this until all 10 cards are given out. The one with the most cards wins.

Talking, reading to your child, and involving them in games that use words and language is the best way to get them learning—and they won't even know it is teaching. And pretty soon they will know half the words on every page in a book.

Index

Acknowledgments

There are so many people to thank after this many years in education. The most important are my thousands of students who taught me, firsthand, what it is really like to have learning differences. They showed me how brilliant they are by working so hard to *succeed*. And succeed they did!

A huge thank you to the teachers and principals who listened during our meetings, made the changes that would most benefit our students, and created more inclusive schools and classes. They understood what I was trying to teach: that students with learning differences were the geniuses of our time.

I want to thank Joan Martin, retired director of Crossroads Elementary School, who asked me to write a report each time I worked with seven-year-old Alex. He became the main inspiration for this book. The reports made me realize I had to be the voice of hope for parents and students.

To the caring, smart parents who worked with me and took steps to ensure the success of their children.

To my forever friends who listened to my student stories for years and gave me the incentive to write what I was doing.

The expertise from my editor, Suzanne Kingsbury, was stellar. Not only her expertise, but her belief that my book was needed and her positive attitude and chanting of "You can do it."

My computer teacher, Sam Bartels, a great teacher who believed that I could actually learn how to use the computer correctly. He has incredible patience.

My illustrator, Carolyn LaPorte, who listened and drew the exact vision I had for the chapter cartoons.

And to Kent Sorsky at Quill Driver Books, whose books I love and who loved this book right away. You are a dream publisher. Thank you for believing in me, my students, and this work.

My husband of 50 years, Marshall, was by my side listening to all my "Dr. Waller" ideas and went along with all of them, even walking with a lion and cheetah in South Africa to show my students.

To my children, Andrew and Alison, and their spouses, Catherine and Jamie, and my wonderful grandchildren, Nick and Julia, who surprise and delight me every day.

About the Author

Victoria E. Waller holds a BS in education from Wayne State University, and both an MEd as a certified reading specialist and an EdD focusing on reading and learning differences from the University of Cincinnati. Dr. Waller was awarded the University of Cincinnati's Distinguished Alumna College of Education Award, was one of three finalists for the LA Music Center's Bravo Award for Outstanding Teaching, and was named a Local Hero in the *Los Angeles Times* for her Printer Pal Program, connecting students with nursing home occupants. She was the creator of the Disney Busy Bags for Travel on Planes and Cars for Disney/Hyperion Books and has created backpacks and toys for Mars, Inc.

Dr. Waller was a founding member of LA's Children's Museum (in operation for 22 years, closing in 2009), was a veteran speaker for the International Reading Association (now the International Literacy Association) for 25 years, and is the focus of *Sixth-Grade Sleepover*, the middle-grade novel by internationally acclaimed Caldecott Medal award winner Eve Bunting. Dr. Waller's articles on creative reading and writing projects for children have been widely viewed on UCLA's Semel Institute for Neuroscience and Human Behavior website and the award-winning Grandparentslink.com.

Dr. Waller and her husband, Marshall, live in Los Angeles, where she has taught all her Labrador retrievers to read with her students. Her latest puppy, Tutor, is still "eating" her books instead of reading them, but she'll learn, eventually! When she isn't teaching students to read and write, Vicki and Marshall travel around the world (70 countries and counting!) to study animals and bring back her knowledge to her students.

To learn more about Dr. Waller, please visit her website at www.drvictoriawaller.com.

CPSIA information can be obtained
at www.ICGtesting.com
Printed in the USA
JSHW051138070622
26609JS00007B/4

9 781610 353861